THE ACEDIAN PIRATES

BY JAY TAYLOR

The Acedian Pirates was first produced by Tara Finney Productions and Theatre503, receiving its world premiere at Theatre503, London, on 26 October 2016.

THE ACEDIAN PIRATES

BY JAY TAYLOR

CAST

Bull	Marc Bannerman
Jacob	Cavan Clarke
Ivan	Matthew Lloyd Davies
Helen	Sheena Patel
Troy	Rowan Polonski
Bernie	Andrew P Stephen

CREATIVE TEAM

Director	Bobby Brook
Designer	Helen Coyston
Lighting Designer	Cat Webb
Composer/Sound Designer	Simon Slater
Movement Director	Mark Conway
Casting Director	Tara Finney
Graphic Designer	Adam Loxley
Photography/Film	Savannah Photographic
Assistant Director	Katie-Ann McDonough
Design Assistant (Intern)	Annie Irving

PRODUCTION TEAM

Producer	Tara Finney Productions & Theatre503
Production Manager	Ben Karakashian
Stage Manager	Lisa Cochrane
Press Representative	Chloé Nelkin Consulting

CAST

MARC BANNERMAN – BULL

Theatre credits include: Shylock in *The Merchant of Venice* (Studio 3 Arts); *In Two Minds* (Theatre Royal, Windsor); *Two Women*, *The Graft* (Theatre Royal, Stratford East); *Absurd Person Singular* (Bill Kenwright tour); *Soap* (Theatre Royal, Northampton).

Marc played popular regular character Gianni di Marco in *EastEnders*. Other TV credits include: *Holby City*, *Coupling*, *Me & Mrs Jones*, *Time Gentlemen Please*, *Dream Team*, *Footballers' Wives: Extra Time* and *Hotel Babylon*.

Film credits include: *Godfathers of London*, *No Reasons*, *The Right to Remain Silent*, *Landscape of Lies*, *Can't Bank on Heaven* and *On the Eight Ball Cortina*.

CAVAN CLARKE – JACOB

Cavan trained at Rose Bruford.

Theatre credits include: *The Plough and the Stars* (National Theatre); *Last of the Boys* (Southwark Playhouse); *Wendy & Peter* (RSC); *Two Noble Kinsmen* (White Bear Theatre); *The Cherry Orchard* (Young Vic); *East of the Sun, West of the Moon* (Quarter Too Ensemble) and *Sleeping Beauty* (The Braids Art Centre/C21).

Film credits include: *Who Will Separate Us*.

MATTHEW LLOYD DAVIES – IVAN

Matthew trained at The Bristol Old Vic Theatre School.

Theatre credits include: *Three Days in the Country, A Small Family Business, The Madness of George III* (National Theatre); *The Taming of the Shrew, Les Liaisons Dangereuses* (RSC); *The Lion King, Chicago, Mamma Mia* (West End/international tour); *The Drowsy Chaperone* (Upstairs at the Gatehouse – nominated Off West End Awards 2010, Best Male); and repertory theatre with Pitlochry, Birmingham, Stoke, Theatr Clwyd, York, Greenwich, Plymouth, Southampton, Northampton.

TV credits include: *Inspector Alleyn, Playing the Field, Wives and Daughters, Shrinks, Over Here, A Rather English Marriage.*

Film credits include: *The Madness of King George, Muppet Treasure Island.*

Radio and Voice credits include: *Mrs Lirriper, Bypassing Jenny, Blind Man's Buff, Puss in Boots.*

Directing credits include: *Wide Awake, Elixir of Love.*

Matthew has also recorded/produced over 75 audiobooks.

SUPPORTERS AND THANKS

The Acedian Pirates **would not have been possible without the support of**

Arts Council England
Nigel & Pauline Taylor
Maddy Brook
Tish Laing Morton
Hilary Mantel
United Agents
Cate Howell
The Peter Woolf Trust
Gugu Mbatha-Raw
Colin Brook
Philip & Chris Carne
Mark Rylance
Henry Brook
Malcolm Sinclair
Hilary Banner
Pippa Kennedy
Denise Gough
Justin Power
Bill Pryde
Joe Murphy
Cas Donald
Mitchell Charlesworth
Peter Eyre
David Rintoul
Milo Twomey
Michael Poulton
Bob & Barbie Low
Christopher Luscombe
Paul Stocker
John Pitt-Brooke
Paul Collyer
Andrew Barrett
Sylvia & Allan
  Rojano-White
Hawkers Cove
Harry Hepple
Pat Orchard
Catherine & Steve Hoare
James Hillier
John Rowe

Migs & Robin Vlies
John Herbertson
Jessica Swale
Grahame & Carole
  Downes
Nick Payne
Pierro Niel-Mee
Michael Shelford
Mark Paszek
Lucy Briers
Al Cruttenden
Matthew Rees
Alex Hanson
Robert Boulter
Ian John Sharp
Josh McGuire
Chad Armstrong
Nick Hendrix
Giles Taylor
Serena Manteghi
Lizzy Watts
Eugene O'Hare
Jon Bonnici
Claire Cox
Andy Payne
Leah Kelbot
Robert & Hilary Pellatt
Paul Jellis
Sebastian Armesto
Nicholas Bishop
David Dawson
Louise Ford
Euan Borland
Gaby Hull
James Bennett
Darren Lane
Emily Barrett
Charlotte Suter-Tibble
Natasha Bradshaw
Laura Keefe
Olivia Darnley
Nellie McQuinn
George Jennings
Rufus Gerrard-Wright
Harry Katsari

Jennie Quirk
Stella Powell-Jones
Justin Audibert
Alistair Cope
Laurel Marks
Court McKenzie
Bridget Barr
Jan & Ian Richardson
Glenys & Ron Shepherd
Charlotte Bird

We would also like to thank

Marston's PLC
George Jennings
Taff Gillingham
Adam Smith
  & Toby Burbidge
Karina Olsen
Joe Kloska
Steve Harper
Natalie Yalden
Lloyd Trott at RADA
Tom Edward-Kane
Cameron Jack
Matti Houghton
Tommy McDonnel'
Pierro Niel-Mee
Justin Salinger
Sope Dirisu
Colm Gormley
John Ramm
Jamie Samu'
Ben Worth
Francesca
Laura Wi'
Adam L'
Paul R'
Lisa, A'
  Au'
  T'

SHEENA PATEL – HELEN

Sheena trained at Guildford School of Acting.

Theatre credits include: *Laila* (Rifco Arts/Watford Palace Theatre); *The Deranged Marriage, Break the Floorboards* (Rifco Arts); *My Big Fat Cowpat Wedding* (Kali); *Wah! Wah! Girls* (Kneehigh/Sadler's Wells); *Robin Hood* (Watford Palace Theatre); *Britain's Got Bhangra* (Rifco Arts/Watford Palace Theatre); *Wuthering Heights* (Tamasha/Lyric Hammersmith); *Miss Lilly Gets Boned* (Osip Theatre/Finborough Theatre); *Romonic* (Soho Theatre) and *In Hearts and Minds* (Khayaal).

Workshop credits include: Gurinder Chada's *Bend It Like Beckham* (West End).

TV credits include: *The Royals* (NBC Universal and Lionsgate); *Emmerdale* (ITV); *EastEnders, Holby City, Law and Order* and *Casualty* (BBC).

ROWAN POLONSKI – TROY

Rowan trained at Rose Bruford.

Theatre credits include: *Desert Rats* (Arts Theatre/Chaskis) and *Another Country* (Trafalgar Studios).

TV credits include: *Doctor Who, Otherworld, Beach Bums* and *The Actors Shrine*.

Film credits include: *The Three of Us* and *Kingsman: The Secret Service*.

ANDREW P STEPHEN – BERNIE

Andrew has appeared in ten seasons of The Cambridge Shakespeare Festival since 1994 in lead roles that include Macbeth, Iago, Angelo, Shylock, Prospero, Petruchio, Benedick, Hamlet and most recently in 2013, Richard III.

West End productions and major tours include: *The Woman in Black* (Fortune/national and Asia tour; he remains the only actor to have played both parts); *Elling* (ATG/Trafalgar Studios); *Absurd Person Singular* (Garrick Theatre/Theatre Royal Bath); *Strangers on a Train* (national tour); *Arsenic and Old Lace* (national tour); *Season's Greetings* (Yvonne Arnaud Theatre); *Funny Peculiar* (national tour) and *Duet for One* (understudy – national tour).

Other Theatre credits include: *Madame Bovary* (The Hope Theatre) and *Foreplay* (King's Head Theatre).

Film credits include: *The Trouble With Dot and Harry* and *The Holt*.

CREATIVES

JAY TAYLOR – WRITER
Jay studied Acting at RADA. He was shortlisted for the 2013 Nick Darke Award for new writing and the 2014 Theatre503 Playwriting Award. *The Acedian Pirates* is Jay's first professional production as a writer.

BOBBY BROOK – DIRECTOR
Bobby is the recipient of a BBC Performing Arts Fund Fellowship, working in-house as Theatre503's Resident Assistant Director in 2014. She has previously worked on both short and feature films for Channel 4, Shoot Productions, Queer as Film and Theatre503.

Directing credits include: *It Never Ends* (Theatre503); *Bold as Brass* (The Duke of Clarence); *Animal Farm, The Book of Everything* (Harrogate Theatre); *Deoxyribonucleic Acid* (National Theatre Connections); *Lily* (Theatre503 Futures) as well as short plays and devised pieces for Theatre503, Tristan Bates Theatre, The Pleasance, Miniaturists and Bits of Obits.

Associate credits include: *My Mother Said I Never Should* (St James Theatre); *Land of Our Fathers* (national tour).

Assistant credits include: *The Life of Stuff* (Theatre503); *Land of Our Fathers, A Handful of Stars* (Theatre503/Trafalgar Studios); *The Women of Troy* (Blue Elephant Theatre); *King Lear* (The Space); *Bus* (West Yorkshire Playhouse); *The Laramie Project, Krapp's Last Tape, The Zoo Story* (Harrogate Theatre).

HELEN COYSTON – DESIGNER
Recent Design credits include: *From the Ground Up* (Almeida Young Company); *Short Changed* (Theatre Royal Plymouth); *My Mother Said I Never Should* (St James Theatre); *The Musicians* (Royal & Derngate, Northampton); *Land of Our Fathers* (Associate Designer, national tour); *Peter Pan, Watership Down, There is a War* (Watford Palace Theatre); *Made Up Stories from my Unmade Bed* (Lyric Hammersmith/Latitude); *1002 Nights* (National Youth Theatre) and *Bluebird* (Edinburgh Fringe). www.helencoyston.com

CAT WEBB – LIGHTING DESIGNER
Catherine designs at the Islington Assembly Rooms, and is also a novelist, writing as herself, Kate Griffin and Claire North. www.catwebblighting.co.uk

Theatre credits include: *Peter Pan, Sleeping Beauty, Sweeney Todd, Aladdin* (Wilde Theatre); *Down and Out in London and Paris* (Pleasance 2/NDT); *Welcome to Thebes, Love and Information, A Clockwork Orange* (Royal & Derngate, Northampton); *Stop! The Play* (Trafalgar Studios 2); *Batboy the Musical* (Southwark Playhouse); *Carousel* (Arcola Theatre); *Dorian Grey* (Riverside Studios); *Crazy Glue* (Pleasance/Assembly Roxy); *Kubrick3* (Pleasance Courtyard); *Love & Money* (ArtsEd); *The Universal Machine, The Dark Room* (NDT); *The Revenge of Sherlock Holmes* (Hoxton Hall); *The Beggar's Opera* (Watermans Arts Centre); *Hot Fudge/Ice Cream* (ArtsEd); *Jekyll and Hyde the Musical* (Union Theatre); *Barbarians, Tinderbox* (Tooting Arts Club); *West Side Story* (Marlowe Theatre, Canterbury); *After the End* (Battersea Arts Centre) and *Theatre Uncut* (Soho Theatre/Latitude).

SIMON SLATER – COMPOSER/SOUND DESIGNER
Simon has composed original music for over 250 theatre, film, television and radio productions. www.slatermusic.com

Theatre credits include: *My Mother Said I Never Should* (St James Theatre); *Untold Stories* (Watermill Theatre); *Deathwatch* (The Print Room); *Bird* (Sherman Theatre Cardiff); *Amadeus* (National Theatre); *Constellations* (Duke of York's Theatre/Royal Court Theatre/ New York, Olivier nominated); *The Winter's Tale* (Sam Wanamaker Playhouse); *Carmen Disruption* (Almeida Theatre); *A Doll's House, Arabian Nights* (Sherman Theatre Cardiff); *Talking Heads* (Theatre Royal Bath/national tour); *The Broken Heart, 'Tis Pity She's a Whore* (Shakespeare's Globe); *Great Expectations* (Vaudeville Theatre); *Octagon* (Arcola Theatre; nominated for Off West End); *The BFG* (Octagon Theatre, Bolton); *Ghosts* (New Vic Theatre); *Single Spies* (Rose Theatre); *Wonderland, Raving, No Naughty Bits, Enlightenment* (Hampstead Theatre); *Land of Our Fathers, Handful of Stars* (Theatre503/ Trafalgar Studios, both Off West End Award nominated); *Cannibals* (Royal Exchange Theatre, Manchester); *Henry V, Julius Caesar, Romeo and Juliet* (RSC); *Macbeth* (Albery Theatre, West End) and *Rose Rage* (Chicago Shakespeare Theatre/Dukes Theatre, New York).

MARK CONWAY – MOVEMENT DIRECTOR
Theatre credits include: *Voyeur: Love Stories* (Southwark Playhouse); *Tiny Tempest* (Brighton Dome); *Land of Our Fathers* (Theatre503/Trafalgar Studios); *Sex With Robots* (Cloakroom Theatre, R&D).

BEN KARAKASHIAN –PRODUCTION MANAGER
Ben graduated from Royal Holloway University of London with a BA Honors in Drama and Theatre Studies.

Production Management credits include: *Frontier Trilogy* (Rabenhof Theatre, Vienna); *Home Chat* (Finborough Theatre); *Titanic the Musical, In the Bar of a Tokyo Hotel, The Mikado* (Charing Cross Theatre); *Kenny Morgan, The Divided Laing* (Arcola Theatre); *The Frontier Trilogy* (Edinburgh Fringe Festival); *The Man Who Shot Liberty Valance* (Park Theatre); *Our Ajax* (Southwark Playhouse); *The Bunker Trilogy* (Southwark Playhouse/Seoul Performing Arts Festival, Stratford Circus).

Stage Management credits include: *Our Ajax, Moment of Truth, Tanzi Libre, Feathers in the Snow* (Southwark Playhouse); *Black Jesus, Soft of Her Palm, The Grand Duke, Goodnight Bird, Portraits, Perchance to Dream* (Finborough Theatre) and *Someone to Blame* (King's Head Theatre).

LISA COCHRANE – STAGE MANAGER
Lisa trained in Professional Production Skills at Guildford School of Acting.

Previous Stage Management credits for Theatre503 include: SM on Book, *And Then Come the Nightjars* (Theatre503/Bristol Old Vic), SM, *WINK* (Theatre503).

Other Theatre credits include: ASM, *Encounters with the Past* (Hampton Court Palace); ASM, *Le Nozze di Figaro and Alcina, Don Pasquale/Rigoletto* (Longborough Festival Opera); SM on Book, *My Mother Said I Never Should* (St James Theatre); SM on Book, *Land of Our Fathers* (Trafalgar Studios/national tour); DSM, *Peter Pan* (Malvern Theatres); DSM, *A Matter of Life & Death* (Electric Theatre Guildford); DSM, *Sleeping Beauty* (Blackpool Grand); SM show cover, *Richard III* (St Paul's Church); DSM, *King Lear* (The Cockpit); SM on Book, *Flesh & Blood Women* (Baby Grand, Belfast Theatre/ tour); PM, *The Kitchen, The Bedroom, and the Grave* (Baby Grand, Belfast Theatre/tour).

KATIE-ANN MCDONOUGH – ASSISTANT DIRECTOR
Theatre credits Include: *Gift Return* (Park Theatre); *Don't Cross Bridges* (Southwark Playhouse); *Ironmistress* (The Albany); *We Grew Up In The Back Of A Van* (White Bear Theatre); *#Nofilter* (Lyric Hammersmith); *You And I Are Earth* (The Vaults).

Tara Finney Productions Ltd

Tara Finney Productions was set up to produce the critically acclaimed *Land of Our Fathers* which was Time Out's *Fringe Show of the Year* when it premiered in September 2013. In March 2015, she produced *WINK* starring *Harry Potter and the Cursed Child* star Sam Clemmett.

This autumn, tfp presents *And Then Come The Nightjars* in collaboration with Theatre503 and Bristol Old Vic, the world premiere of Theatre503 Playwriting Award finalist *The Acedian Pirates* and is acting as general manager for Interval Productions' new musical *Muted* in The Bunker Theatre's inaugural season. In spring 2017, tfp is producing the world premiere of Arinze Kene's new play *good dog* for tiata fahodzi and Watford Palace Theatre.

Theatre credits include:

- *The Acedian Pirates* (Theatre503); Finalist Theatre503 Playwriting Award 2014

- *And Then Come The Nightjars* (national tour); nominated for UK Theatre Award 2016 Best Design; shortlisted Susan Smith Blackburn Award 2015; winner Theatre503 Playwriting Award 2014

- *WINK* (Theatre503); nominated for Off West End Awards 2015 Best New Play, Most Promising New Playwright, Best Director, Best Sound Designer

- *Land of Our Fathers* (Found111, national tour, Trafalgar Studios, Theatre503); nominated for Off West End Awards 2014 Best New Play, Best Production; Finalist, Best Director, Best Set Designer, Best Lighting Designer

tarafinney.com
@tara_finney
facebook.com/tarafinneyproductions
instagram.com/tarafinneyproductions

TARA FINNEY – PRODUCER

Tara qualified as a corporate solicitor before starting her theatrical career as Resident Assistant Producer at Theatre503 in May 2012. She then worked as Producer for Iris Theatre and as Associate Producer at Company of Angels, before going freelance full time in July 2015. Tara recently launched new production company Tiny Fires with director Paul Robinson and their inaugural production, *My Mother Said I Never Should* starring Maureen Lipman and Katie Brayben, received critical acclaim during its run at St James Theatre in spring 2016 – www.tinyfires.co.uk. Tara is supported by the Stage One Bursary Scheme.

Other Theatre credits include: *My Mother Said I Never Should* (St James Theatre); *World Factory* (Young Vic/New Wolsey Theatre); Theatre Café Woolwich (Greenwich & Lewisham Young People's Theatre); *Helver's Night* (York Theatre Royal); *Alice Through the Looking Glass, Richard III* (St Paul's Church); *Respect, Buy Nothing Day* (ALRA Studio), *I, Peaseblossom / I, Caliban* (national tour); Theatre Café York (York Theatre Royal); *Alice in Wonderland, Julius Caesar* (St Paul's Church); *Desolate Heaven, Where the Mangrove Grows, ELEGY, Life for Beginners* (Theatre503); *Bluebird* (Bedlam, Courtyard, South Hill Park).

ROBYN BENNETT – ASSISTANT PRODUCER

Robyn previously worked as an agent's assistant before undertaking the Resident Assistant Producer scheme at Theatre503. Currently a freelance theatre producer, Robyn has been shortlisted for the Old Vic 12 and is producing a revival of James Bridie's *Dr Angelus* at the Finborough Theatre this winter.

Theatre credits include: *Screens* (as associate,Theatre503); *Clickbait, Four Play, BU21, We Wait In Joyful Hope* (as assistant,Theatre503); *Your Ever Loving* (as associate, Theatre N16); *The State We're In* (Theatre503).

ELLIE PARKER – PRODUCTION ASSISTANT (INTERN)

Ellie has just finished sixth form at Abbey Gate College and is taking a gap year before going to study Geography at Newcastle University. During her gap year she is aiming to travel to as many places as possible – including India, Sri Lanka, Namibia and Thailand – whilst also gaining work experience in theatre and performance which she is very passionate about.

THEATRE503

Theatre503 is the award-winning home of groundbreaking plays.

Led by Artistic Director Lisa Spirling, Theatre503 is a flagship new writing venue committed to producing bold, brave new plays. We are the smallest theatre in the world to win an Olivier award and we offer more opportunities to new writers than any other theatre in the UK.

THEATRE503 TEAM

Artistic Director	Lisa Spirling
Executive Director	Andrew Shepherd
Producer	Jessica Campbell
Literary Manager	Steve Harper
Literary Coordinators	Lauretta Barrow, Nika Obydzinski
Office Manager	Anna De Freitas
Resident Assistant Producers	Bridget Rudder, Audrey Thayer
Senior Readers	Kate Brower, Rob Young

THEATRE503 BOARD

Royce Bell, Peter Benson, Chris Campbell, Kay Ellen Consolver, Ben Hall, Dennis Kelly, Eleanor Lloyd, Marcus Markou, Geraldine Sharpe-Newton, Jack Tilbury, Erica Whyman (Chair), Roy Williams.

THEATRE503 HEROES

These brilliant volunteers give their valuable time and expertise to Theatre503 as front of house and box office managers, script readers and much more.

Alice Mason, Anna Middlemass, Anna Mors, Anna Landi, Andrei Vornicu, Asha Osborne, Annabel Pemberton, Bethany Doherty, Brett Westwell, Carla Grauls, Carla Kingham, Cecilia Garcia, Cecily King, Chelsey Gillard, Charlotte Mulliner, Chidi Chukwu, Damian Robertson, Danielle Wilson,D avid Benedictus, Dominic Jones, Elena Valentine, Emma Brand, Fabienne Gould, George Linfield, Gillian Greer, Imogen Robertson, Isla Coulter, James Hansen, Jim Mannering, Joanna Lallay, Joe Ackerman, Joel Ormsby, Kate Brower, Kelly Agredo, Ken Hawes, Larner Taylor, Lisa Cagnacci, Lucy Atkins, Maddy Ryle, Mandy Nicholls, Mark Doherty, Martin Edwards, Michelle Sewell, Mike McGarry, Nathalie Czarnecki, Nick Cheesman, Nicole Marie Bartlett, Paul Webb, Rahim Dhanji, Rebecca Latham, Reetu Sood, Rob Ellis, Saul Reid, Serafina Cusack, Sevan Greene, Simon Mander, Stephanie de Whalley, Stuart Quinn, Tamsin Irwin, Tess Hardy, Tim Bano, Tobias Chapple, Tom Hartwell, Tom Latter, Tommo Fowler, Valeria Bello, Valeria Montesano, Vanessa Garcia, Will Callaghan, Yasmeen Arden.

THEATRE503 IS SUPPORTED BY

Angela Hyde-Courtney, Cas Donald, Francesca Ortona, Georgia Oetker, Geraldine Sharpe-Newton, Gregory Dunlop, Katherine Malcom, Philip and Chris Carne, Stephanie Knauf, Sumintra Latchman.

SUPPORT THEATRE503

Help us take risks on new writers and produce the plays that other theatres can't, or won't. Together we can discover the writers of tomorrow and make some of the most exciting theatre in the country. With memberships ranging from £23 to £1003 you can get involved no matter what your budget, to help us remain 'arguably the most important theatre in Britain today' (*Guardian*).

Benefits range from priority notice of our work and news, access to sold out shows, ticket deals, and opportunities to peek into rehearsals. Visit **theatre503.com** or call **020 7978 7040** for more details.

VOLUNTEER WITH US

There are many ways to get involved in Theatre503, from joining our reading team to assisting during technical weeks or working front of house. If you're interested in volunteering please email **volunteer@theatre503.com**

Theatre503, 503 Battersea Park Rd, London, SW11 3BW I 020 7978 7040 I theatre503.com I @theatre503 I Facebook.com/theatre503

THE ACEDIAN PIRATES

Jay Taylor

To Mum and Dad,
with love and thanks
xx

Characters

HELEN
JACOB
IVAN
BULL
BERNIE
TROY

Setting

A lighthouse.

Time

Possibly the future, possibly the past.

This text went to press before the end of rehearsals and so may differ slightly from the play as performed.

ACT ONE

Scene One

Choral music. Sombre and ominous.

A single light picks out a woman stood centre stage. She is
HELEN.

HELEN*'s body is bruised and bloodied, particularly around her
wrists and ankles, and she has scratch marks all over her.*

A group of men walk slowly on to the stage and stand observing
HELEN *with an almost religious devotion.*

HELEN. Tell me a story.

Beat.

Tell me. A story.

Beat.

No? Then I'll tell you mine.

Beat.

They came from across the sea when I was but a little girl;
one who would sit and play and tangle her hair in wreaths of
ringlets. They came with gifts. They came with smiles. They
came with HIM.

Beat.

I felt his cold eyes upon me. My father knew. No one knows
an evil man's mind better than another evil man. He
poisoned everyone with his words. I was intended for
another, but I knew that he would make me his. It was
simply a matter of time.

Beat.

I was dreaming when they came for me, dreaming that I had
angel wings, that I could fly far and away and above and up.
My dreams took me far above their pitched tents and

battlements, away from him and his men of clutch, of fist; men of angry promises.

Beat.

But in the darkness they came and I was awakened, stolen and like a wretched animal, dragged through the desert, not screaming; silent. Or rather, screaming in silence and when finally we reached this place, his face was no surprise to me.

Beat.

But soon another shall come. And so I wait. And in moments of peace, precious and rare that they are, I think of days gone by. Of a little girl who sits and plays and tangles her hair in wreaths of ringlets and dreams of having angel wings. She isn't anyone, but she is everything. Everything to men of nothing.

The music fractures and distorts; it becomes heavy, rhythmic, militaristic.

The music grows and incorporates a soundscape of shouts, screaming, panic, terror, war.

Blackout.

Scene Two

A lighthouse.

The sound of the ocean.

The music cuts out and lights snap up on two men dressed in military attire.

JACOB paces, a book in his hand, smoking heavily.

IVAN sits, drinking.

Muffled noise, like stifled cries, come from above them.

They both look up.

A pause.

JACOB. You gonna do something?

IVAN. Like what?

The men look at each other.

JACOB. I'll call them again.

IVAN. There's no word.

JACOB. You're sure?

IVAN. Has the phone rung since the last time I checked?

JACOB. No.

IVAN. Well, there you have it then.

JACOB. Right.

IVAN. Why don't you sit down.

JACOB. Why are you so obsessed with sitting down?

IVAN. I'm hardly 'obsessed'.

JACOB. You never used to be a sitting-down type of bloke.
Certainly not at a time like this.

IVAN. A time like what?

JACOB. A time like *this*.

IVAN. Well, I'm just… giving it a go. A trial run.

JACOB. Right.

IVAN. Yeah.

JACOB. And?

IVAN. And what?

JACOB. And, what's it like?

IVAN. Sitting down?

JACOB. Yeah.

IVAN. It's comfortable, isn't it.

JACOB. Right.

   A pause.

   The conversation has taken a somewhat peculiar turn.

IVAN. Well. War's a peculiar business.

JACOB. It is.

   Beat.

   I'm just surprised to see you looking so… *composed*, is all,
   Ivan.

IVAN. Composed? I'm just taking a load off. Good for the feet.
   Personally, I can't comprehend people who stand up all the
   time. Not when there's a perfectly good seat to sit on.

JACOB. Oh no?

IVAN. A great leader was once asked what the secret to living
   a long life was. He said, 'Never stand up when you can sit
   down and never *sit down* when you can *lie down*.'

JACOB. Hmm.

IVAN. You see them, though, don't you. Five people in the
   whole place, seats aplenty and they're *stood*. God gave us
   our own portable cushions in the shape of the humble
   buttocks, yet still some people stand there all vertical and…
   stood. To me that's just fucking madness, Jacob.

JACOB. I suppose so.

IVAN. But that's just me.

Pause.

IVAN *looks pointedly at an empty chair.*

JACOB *slowly sits in the empty chair.*

JACOB (*getting up suddenly*). Maybe I should go up there.

IVAN (*sharp*). JACOB!

JACOB *stops.*

You're not going up there.

JACOB. Oh no?

IVAN. NO. You're not going up there.

JACOB (*sotto*). Look, I appreciate everything you've done for me but...

IVAN. I'll explain everything in good time, but for now... just do as I say.

JACOB *puts his cigarette out.*

IVAN *finishes his drink.*

Sit down.

JACOB. No.

IVAN. Have a drink.

JACOB. No.

IVAN. Have another cigarette then.

A pause.

JACOB. Alright.

JACOB *lights another cigarette.*

IVAN *pours another drink.*

IVAN. You smoke too much.

JACOB. Yeah, well, you drink too much.

IVAN. Oh is that so?

JACOB. Yes, it is.

IVAN. We all have our vices.

JACOB. It would seem so.

IVAN. But then… maybe it's your thing, eh? The smokes. Maybe that's your… *hobby*.

JACOB. It's a cigarette, not a fucking yo-yo.

IVAN. The mouth on him. To a superior officer.

JACOB. With respect, *sir*, I'll stop smoking when you've stopped sweating single malt.

IVAN goes to say something but stops.

He pours a little water into his whisky glass.

IVAN. Touché, fuckpig.

JACOB. *Fuckpig?*

IVAN. Fuckpig.

JACOB looks a little bit hurt.

JACOB. That's a bit strong.

IVAN. Everyone has to cope.

IVAN looks at his glass of whisky.

In their own way.

JACOB. Right.

IVAN. As I say… we all have our vices.

JACOB. Mmm.

(*Gesturing upstairs.*) Even her?

They both look up.

IVAN. We'll find out soon enough.

Beat.

What you reading?

JACOB *tosses his book to* IVAN. IVAN *looks unimpressed. He squints.*

(*Reading*.) 'We that stood idle when evil deeds were done. Now we are sullen in the black mire of acedia.'

IVAN *looks up at* JACOB.

Comedy, is it?

JACOB (*thinking*). Of sorts. I'll let you know.

IVAN. Can't wait.

IVAN *goes to read more of the book.*

Eyesight's bad. Must be the light.

JACOB. Must be.

IVAN (*squinting*). Could be the size of the print, though...

JACOB. Could be the attritional ageing process.

Beat.

I can see for miles.

IVAN. Oh really?

JACOB. Yep.

IVAN. Can you see this?

IVAN *sticks two fingers up.*

JACOB. That's not very nice.

IVAN. Awfully sorry. The 'attritional ageing process' has made me somewhat *cantankerous*.

Beat.

You wait till your eyes start to go.

JACOB *smiles.*

Here, I knew a chap once. Went on to do... terrible things. Became a fascist. A dictator.

JACOB. A fascist dictator then?

IVAN *looks unimpressed.* JACOB *shrugs.*

IVAN. We served together before he was… as infamous as all that. He was a regular soldier. Spit and polish, just like us. Anyway, he and I wound up at a medical facility together. He had mild gas poisoning, I had a… relatively innocuous but somewhat concerning virus…

JACOB. What sort of virus…?

IVAN. That's not the point of the story. *Anyway*… this chap, he'd been gassed. Not badly, not a life-threatening injury, still…

JACOB. Still… gas is gas.   IVAN. Gas is gas.

IVAN. Exactly. And this fella, he'd lost his eyesight. Naturally, they made the assumption that it was as a result of exposure to the gas…

JACOB. Nasty.

IVAN. Very nasty. But they realised… after a period of… consultation… that there was nothing wrong with his eyes. His eyes… were fine. Unaffected by the gas. In A-one working order.

JACOB. Then why couldn't he see?

IVAN. Ah. Hysterical blindness.

JACOB. You what?

IVAN. Hysterical blindness. It was all in his head.

JACOB. All in his head?

IVAN. All in his head. Shell shocked.

JACOB. Shell shocked?

IVAN. What are you, a fucking parrot?

JACOB *looks confused.*

JACOB. Carry on.

IVAN. His eyesight returned. After *psychological* treatment. No medicine. Just words.

The doctor that treated him taught him a very important lesson; he taught him that the strength of his will and personal conviction could bring him to recovery. That soldier realised how powerful the mind could be.

Beat.

Good story, isn't it?

A pause.

JACOB. Huh. Makes you wonder...

IVAN. Wonder what?

JACOB. Well... if the doctor hadn't have cured him. If he'd somehow known what the future held...

IVAN. He was a doctor, not a fucking soothsayer.

JACOB. No I know... but that doctor... he cured a man who went on to terrible things. What would have happened if he hadn't cured him?

IVAN. Wouldn't have made no difference.

JACOB. Even though he was an invalid? Would a blind man still have been able to brainwash and coerce all those people?

IVAN. A doctor has an obligation. To cure people. They take an oath thing...

JACOB. I know. But I'm saying... in that scenario... with knowledge of what the consequences were...

Beat.

It's a dichotomy. It's a dichotomy.

IVAN. You and your fucking dichotomies. You ain't changed a bit.

They laugh.

A pause.

JACOB. It is a good story though.

IVAN. I know it's a good story, that's why I told you it. And now you can tell it to someone and pretend it's *your* story.

JACOB. Is that what you did?

IVAN smiles.

You weren't in hospital with him, were you.

IVAN. Works better if I was. Stories should always be told in the first person.

JACOB. I see.

JACOB looks up.

Do you know what *her* name is? For when I tell *this* story. I am in the intelligence division, now...

IVAN (*dangerously*). This ain't a story you wanna tell, mate. Believe me.

A stifled scream from upstairs.

JACOB and IVAN look up, then back at each other.

A pause.

Look, the less you know... the better. That's how we do things in intelligence.

JACOB. Right.

Beat.

I've got to be honest, that somewhat contradicts my understanding of the word *intelligence*.

IVAN. I don't want you compromised. You need to maintain... plausible deniability.

If you don't know nothing... you can't say nothing, can you.

JACOB. Right.

IVAN. Some of the lads. The ones who brought her here... they saw her. They were... *compromised*.

JACOB. And?

IVAN. And they're not here having a fag and a dichotomy, are they.

JACOB considers this.

JACOB. Have you ever seen her?

IVAN *scoffs*.

IVAN. Course I have.

JACOB. What's she like?

IVAN. She's... well... I mean, if you're asking have I myself actually set my own eyes on her, then technically speaking, no... I suppose I haven't. But I know lots of people who have.

JACOB. Right. And... did these people find out her name?

IVAN. Let's just call her... Helen.

JACOB. Helen. Right.

Two men suddenly enter the room.

BERNIE *is small, precise and calculating. He wears a more elaborate uniform than the others, denoting seniority of rank.*

BULL *is large, stern and physically intimidating. He is dressed in the same style as* JACOB *and* IVAN.

BERNIE. Ivan.

IVAN *embraces* BERNIE *as an old friend.*

BULL *closes the door and stands guard, arms folded.*

JACOB *stands to attention.*

BERNIE *looks up nervously.*

She up there?

IVAN *nods*.

BERNIE *loosens his tie and immediately makes himself at home.*

Right. Well. There's no word yet, okay. There's nothing. Not yet. But there will be and when we get the word we have to be ready to move. Pronto. On the double. I expect absolute attention and diligence to duty at all times. The end is in sight, gentlemen. This is the final step. Let's not lose our footing now.

Clear?

ALL. Clear.

BERNIE. I appreciate you being here, gentlemen, really I do. We are on high alert. Everyone understand what that means?

ALL. Sir.

BERNIE. Now. The operation was successful and for that I think we can all be very grateful. There could've been issues. Unfortunate issues. And I'm not inclined to comment on what these issues could've been, but suffice to say, I am very glad that we are now…

BERNIE *loses his train of thought.*

IVAN. Issue-free.

BERNIE (*quickly*). Issue-free. Thank you, Ivan. It was a delicate situation and the appropriate… measures… have been taken. Measures and precautions. You understand? Bull?

BULL. Yes, sir.

BERNIE. Ivan?

IVAN. Yes, Bernie. I understand.

BERNIE (*looking* JACOB *up and down*). And how about you?

JACOB. Yes, I understand, Bernie.

BULL, IVAN *and* BERNIE *murmur their disapproval.*

BULL. Oh dear.

IVAN. Sorry about that, Bernie.

BERNIE. It's okay, Ivan.

(*To* JACOB.) You do not address me by my forename. I am yet to introduce myself to you in a personal capacity. You are only aware of what my forename is because my friend Ivan here just addressed me in that fashion, which he is well within his rights to do, he being an old friend and long-time colleague of mine. I find your presumption very offensive, if I'm quite honest, young man.

JACOB. Sorry. I meant no offence. It's just over the other side we…

BERNIE. Oh the '*other side*', eh?

BULL, IVAN *and* BERNIE *scoff derisively and mutter obscenities.*

JACOB. Er... how should I...

BERNIE. Sir. You call me 'sir'. Sir is how you should address me until further notice.

JACOB. Yes, sir. I apologise.

BERNIE. Apology accepted. Name?

JACOB. Jacob, sir.

BERNIE. Jacob. So. From the other side of the island, are you?

JACOB. Yes, sir. Just got transferred. Arrived last night.

BERNIE. Well, I don't know how they do things over '*the other side*', but this side... we like to keep a certain amount of decorum. Do you know what decorum means?

JACOB. Yes, sir. I do.

BERNIE. And I gather you're an old family friend of Ivan's, come to work with us in intelligence? That right?

JACOB. That's right, sir.

BERNIE. Intelligence is a vital part of our operation. It's no laughing matter. Unless of course you have a distinct *lack* of intelligence, in which case I should think you should find *everything* a laughing matter.

BERNIE *does a sharp, loud laugh at his own joke, that ends as abruptly as it started.*

You're not two spanners short of a toolbox, though, are you, boy?

JACOB. No, sir.

BERNIE. Hmm. Right.

Beat.

Let's have a drink.

IVAN *pours some drinks.*

Bull, will you take a drink?

BULL. I will. Thank you, sir.

    BERNIE *hands* BULL *a drink.*

BERNIE (*to* JACOB). Hear that? 'Sir.' Decorum. Respect. Bull here is one of our best. A fine individual. Very fine. I selected him to be my personal aide because of his...

    BERNIE *looks* BULL *up and down and licks his lips slightly.*

    ...*physical attributes.* But also because of his humility and sense of place.

    Isn't that right, Mr Bull?

BULL. That's right, sir.

BERNIE. Plus he has an excellent sense of humour, isn't that right, Mr Bull.

BULL. That's right, sir.

    BERNIE, IVAN *and* BULL *laugh uproariously.* JACOB *looks confused.*

BERNIE (*stops laughing suddenly*). Do you have an excellent sense of humour, young man?

JACOB. I like to think so, sir.

BERNIE. Oh do you indeed?

IVAN. Oh he does. Young Jacob here, he's quite the prankster. Very witty with it, too.

BERNIE. Is he now?

IVAN. And he's a FANTASTIC mimic.

BERNIE. Mimic? Is he really?

IVAN. Just this afternoon he was doing a very well-observed impression of Mr Bull here, weren't you, Jacob?

JACOB (*confused*). What...

BERNIE. Oh wonderful! Well, I'd very much like to see that and I'm sure Mr Bull would too, wouldn't you, Mr Bull.

BULL. Indeed I would, sir.

BULL stands very close to JACOB.

JACOB looks very confused and scared.

IVAN and BERNIE stare intently at him.

A pause.

IVAN, BERNIE and BULL all suddenly break the tension and laugh.

BERNIE. Look at the face on him! Oh dear, we're only pulling your leg, son!

IVAN. Sorry, Jacob. Just a little initiation we like to do.

JACOB breathes a sigh of relief and nervously goes to light another cigarette.

BERNIE (*suddenly very serious*). Smokes a lot, don't he.

The other three all stare at JACOB.

IVAN. He does.

A pause.

BERNIE. Maybe that's his   BULL. Could be his thing…?
thing, though.

IVAN. That's what I said.

JACOB takes the unlit cigarette out of his mouth and puts it back in the pack.

They all stare at him.

JACOB. Sir, I just want to say that it's a great privilege to be serving here. I'm very grateful to yourself and to Ivan for… easing my transition into intelligence, sir.

BERNIE. Ah, there we go. Respect. Very good.

BERNIE pats JACOB on the back.

We're glad to have you. We need every good man we can muster.

JACOB. It's true then, sir? That… it's nearly over. That we… might be going home.

A pause. The others all share a look.

BERNIE. Home?

Muffled talking from upstairs. A man shouting aggressively. They all look up.

(*To* IVAN.) Up there, is he?

IVAN. Yeah. Course he his. Never leaves her side, does he. He's somewhat of a permanent fixture. Like a light switch.

BERNIE. Except he don't turn off.

IVAN. Well…

BERNIE. *Home*, eh? Home. Depends… depends on a lot of things. The sea, for one. The weather systems. The tide.

JACOB. The moon, sir.

They all stare at JACOB.

BERNIE *walks to the window and looks out.*

BERNIE. Quiet out there now. Very quiet. But when we came over… my word. Remember, Bull.

BULL. Certainly do, sir.

BERNIE. Waves like cliff faces. Crashing, rolling. Relentless. The power of them… quite a sight to behold.

IVAN. The old boys made it… long time ago, but things weren't so different then.

BERNIE. The old boys… yes. True. But don't be deceived by that calm. The ocean is a cruel mistress.

Beat.

It's like a fight. The quietest man in the room is always the most dangerous.

BERNIE *laughs, attempting to lighten the mood.*

But… if the old boys made it, why can't we?

BULL. Indeed, sir.

BERNIE. A long time we've been away. A lot of good men we've lost. But we've made progress. Yes?

IVAN. Oh, yes.

BULL. Definitely, sir.

IVAN. Upheld the traditions of the Capital State.

A pause.

BERNIE *frowns.*

BERNIE. Indeed. Progress. We've helped people. We've furthered the cause. Done some good.

BERNIE *goes to say more, but decides to keep his counsel.*

Nevertheless, young man. You join us at a very precarious point in our campaign. I hope we can rely on you to do your bit. You're here to assist. That's what we do.

JACOB. Yes, sir.

BERNIE. Good.

A phone rings, making JACOB *jump.*

They all stare at it for a time.

JACOB. The telephone's ringing.

BERNIE *and* IVAN *look at each other.*

BERNIE (*to* IVAN). Fuck me, I'm glad we've got him in intelligence.

BERNIE *gestures to* IVAN, *who picks up the receiver.*

IVAN (*into phone*). Hello? Yes. Right.

Beat.

I see. Okay. Thank you.

IVAN *puts the phone down.*

They need some help down at the docks. I'll go. Could do with stretching me legs, anyway.

BERNIE. How close are they?

IVAN. No sightings as yet.

BERNIE. Well, stay sharp. You know what they're like.

IVAN. Sir.

BERNIE. Mr Bull, you go with him. Jacob lad, you stay here.

Beat.

Get to know each other properly, eh?

JACOB. Sir.

BULL *and* IVAN *exit.*

A pause.

Do you mind if I smoke, sir? I'm trying to cut down, but…

BERNIE. Course I don't mind, son. Smoke away. We were only teasing you before.

You shouldn't be so sensitive.

Beat.

Mind you, sensitivity is a rare trait in a young man. I like people who are sensitive. People who think about things.

JACOB. I do think about things, sir.

BERNIE. Do you, boy?

JACOB. I think about home.

BERNIE. Yes. A man should miss his home. A man who doesn't isn't happy when he's there. I feel like I can hardly remember it, now. Been a long time since we came here. A lot's changed.

Beat.

We arrived in glory. Treated like the heroes we are. Sent here by the mighty Capital State to salvage some dignity for the oppressed, to stand up against terror and evil.

Beat.

But… soon we leave.

JACOB. You don't think we should, sir?

BERNIE *stares at* JACOB *and lowers his voice.*

BERNIE. Can I trust you, Jacob?

JACOB. Yes, sir.

BERNIE. Because these are dangerous times.

JACOB *nods.*

Nobody wants to see an end to this bloody war more than I do. It's... the *manner* in which we're leaving.

Beat.

It's the end of an age, you know. An end to the age of heroes, as they say...

BERNIE *looks up.*

All for her.

JACOB. Is she really worth it, sir?

BERNIE. She *has* to be.

Beat.

She... *is*... the war now. You understand?

JACOB *nods.*

BERNIE *softens and smiles.*

You got a girl back home? Someone waiting for you?

Good-looking boy, you are...

JACOB. Not really, sir.

BERNIE. Ah, well. You make sure that you know some women... or men, if that's your...

JACOB (*firm*). No. It's not. Sir.

BERNIE. Whatever slings your shot, as they say.

Men... women... none of my business.

JACOB. Have you... known a lot of women in your life, sir?

BERNIE. Oohhhhh.

BERNIE and JACOB *share a laugh.*

Enough. Enough for me.

JACOB. How do you know how many is enough?

BERNIE. You just do. And it's different for everyone.

I had my fun. As a younger man I was up the scallyhouses every night of the week. A visit to the Madam once before breakfast and again after dinner. Regular as clockwork. Like taking pills after a meal. Which… quite a few of us had to do…

BERNIE looks a little embarrassed.

There was a… relatively innocuous but rather concerning virus going around at the time…

JACOB. I see.

BERNIE (*covering*). But whilst I'm not condoning an amoral attitude towards fornication… it's important not to have any regrets. Regret is a terrible thing.

A noise from above. They both look up.

A terrible thing.

A pause.

JACOB. Have *you* seen her, sir?

BERNIE. You mean…

BERNIE points upstairs.

JACOB nods.

BERNIE winks, nods and laughs ambiguously.

JACOB laughs and winks back.

Well, not exactly no.

JACOB. Ah.

BERNIE. But I tell you this. She's…

BERNIE *simply exhales and smiles*.

She's the moon.

JACOB *nods*.

Or so they say.

A pause.

JACOB. Over the other side, you see... they all talk and tell stories about her. Stories about what she means to us. But I always thought they were just...

BERNIE (*enjoying the word*). A-poc-ry-phal?

JACOB. Exactly, sir. Exactly. But then... after a while, you can't help but start to believe them. And now... suddenly I'm here. And she's here too. And we're supposed to sit tight and keep watch and wait for the word, but... I just don't understand...

Muffled screams and a man's voice from upstairs.

Sir, what is it that he's trying to...

BERNIE. Careful.

Beat.

It's an interrogation. It's complicated. It's a lengthy process.

JACOB. But sir, with respect...

BERNIE *gets up suddenly, walks over to* JACOB *and violently grabs him*.

BERNIE. You listen to me. You keep your mouth shut and your eyes down. Clear? You do your duty and we might get home.

BERNIE *lets* JACOB *go*.

JACOB *nods ashamedly*.

BERNIE *softens and pats* JACOB *on the shoulder*.

Look... I'm sorry, son. I've heard the stories. But you have to understand what's at stake here.

Beat.

Her lot have raised flags against us. That means they're coming. And we don't have the men to…

Beat.

When we leave, we're never coming back. You're enthusiastic. Full of questions. I like that, I like that very much. But there are questions you don't ask.

JACOB. Sir.

BERNIE. You talk to me, you talk to Ivan and you talk to Bull.

A man laughs upstairs.

Nobody else.

JACOB. Sorry, sir.

BERNIE. Don't be sorry. Just be smart.

BERNIE *looks at his watch in frustration and then goes to the window.*

Where are they?

Beat.

I'm sorry if I'm being hard on you, boy. It's all this talk of… *abduction…*

JACOB (*under his breath*). Raptus.

BERNIE. Eh?

JACOB. Raptus.

BERNIE *goes to say something as* BULL *re-enters.*

BULL. Sir?

BERNIE. What is it?

BULL. I think you'd better come down, sir. They need your authorisation for a few things.

BERNIE. Just when I'm getting settled. Right, come on then. (*To* JACOB.) You remember what we talked about, boy. Decorum. *Duty.* Yes?

JACOB *nods.*

BERNIE *stares at him.*

Good boy. Good boy.

BERNIE *and* BULL *exit.*

JACOB *paces. He sits and resumes reading his book.*

A lighting change.

Music.

Scene Three

JACOB *alone, reading.*

He stands up and stretches.

The upstairs door opens and TROY *enters, unseen by* JACOB. *He is shirtless, muscular and barefoot. He is both terrifying and utterly charismatic in equal measure.*

He observes JACOB *for a time.*

TROY. Who are you?

JACOB *immediately stands to attention.*

JACOB. Jacob, sir.

TROY. Where's Ivan? Left us, has he? Deserted?

JACOB. He was wanted down at the docks.

TROY. I see.

TROY *yawns and mooches about the room.*

No word?

JACOB. Not yet, sir.

TROY. Hmm.

Beat.

Do you like it here?

JACOB. I only arrived last night, sir.

TROY. Oh yeah.

Beat.

You seen a lighthouse before?

JACOB. Once, sir.

TROY. Funny little places, aren't they?

TROY *looks around the room.*

They warn you: 'Don't go near that. That's dangerous.' It's like a person, isn't it? That's what people like to do. Warn.

JACOB. I suppose so, sir. Yes.

TROY. Cos they think that they know best.

JACOB. Yes, sir.

TROY. Oh yeah. See… there are two certainties that the average human has to come to terms with: death, and the fact that every cunt you meet thinks that they could live your life a lot better than the way that you live it.

Beat.

Now, that's a fact. But we're all fucking psychologists when it comes to giving advice, aren't we?

Beat.

When someone says to me, 'in my opinion' or 'take my advice', I give them a good fucking slap. A stinger. A cheek-scorcher. Man or woman. It may seem a little effeminate for a man to deal another man an open-handed blow, granted, but it's not a situation that really warrants a proper clump, nor can the imposition go unanswered. Do you find that an appropriate response?

JACOB. Yes, sir.

TROY. So do I, Jacob. Yet I often find that the recipient of the slap disagrees.

TROY *stares at* JACOB.

JACOB. Maybe… they think they're doing you a favour, sir.

TROY. That's right! But they're not, are they. Self-interest,
that's what it is.

Beat.

Tell you a story. I popped along to the church one day,
ducked into the old confessional, just for a laugh, like. 'Tell
me your sins, child,' the geezer says, 'My sins? I can't do
that, Father,' says I. 'God listens and he doesn't judge, child,'
says he. So I tell him my sins. I tell him all of it. In depth,
with accuracy and in vivid reconstructive detail. I paint a
picture, with every nuance of every sin I've ever committed.
And that's a fucking story, I can tell you.

A pause.

Anyway. This priest. He… well, he didn't seem to enjoy my
little memoir. He tried to *eject* me, Jacob. And I was happy
to leave until he uttered the fateful words, 'Take it from
me…' So I gave him a lovely hard slap, right across his fat
fucking chops. He was so shocked he fell over and pissed
himself.

A pause.

But then… do you know what he says to me? Do you know
what word this… this 'man of God' calls me? 'Wicked.' He
calls me a 'wicked child'. He starts clovering on about my
soul and all this spiritual crump about the wretched raging
fires of hell and eternal damnation. I say to him. 'Hang on…
what about FORGIVENESS? Isn't that what this is all
about? Confess and thou shalt be forgiven?' But 'No,' he
says… 'forgiveness is only to redeem the soul. Those
without a soul cannot be saved.'

Beat.

That's me fucked then.

TROY *laughs.*

TROY *stops laughing.*

You religious?

JACOB. I don't know, sir.

TROY. Don't know, eh? Agnostic, they call that.

JACOB. Sir.

TROY. Undecided.

JACOB. I suppose so, sir.

TROY. Take my word for it, Jacob... there's nothing. *Nothing*.
So make the most of this life while you've got it.

JACOB. Sir.

TROY. Been here long?

JACOB. Yes, sir. Over the other side, though, sir.

TROY. The '*other side*', eh?

JACOB. Yes, sir... you see...

TROY. Why won't you look at me?

JACOB. I'm sorry, sir?

TROY. Look me in the eye.

JACOB *does so, reluctantly*.

TROY *looks at him*.

What's your opinion? About all this.

A pause.

TROY *smiles*.

Hmm. Right then.

BERNIE, BULL *and* IVAN *enter and immediately stiffen at
the sight of* TROY. *They treat him with the same deference
you would give a dangerous wild animal*.

Bernie. Any word?

BERNIE. Not yet, sir. Nothing, no. You'll be the first to know
when we hear, sir. I can assure you of that.

TROY. Right.

BERNIE. We were just down at the docks, sir.

TROY. So young Jacob here tells me. We've just been having a little chat. Haven't we, Jacob?

JACOB. Sir.

IVAN. I'm sorry for any offence he may have caused, sir.

TROY. Offence?

IVAN. Yes. He's that type, sir.

TROY. Oh he is, is he?

IVAN. He's a good boy. But he's got ideas, you see.

BERNIE. Oh yes. Lots of ideas. I just hope he showed you all due respect, sir.

TROY *sits down and puts his boots on.*

We were just talking about respect and decorum before we left, weren't we, Jacob? I trust he conducted himself... appropriately, sir.

TROY. Well. Decorum is all good and well, Bernie, but we *need* men with ideas. Men of industry.

A pause.

If we're ever going to get home... men with ideas could be very important.

The others all look at TROY *nervously.*

TROY *starts to leave.*

Bull! Didn't see you there! How you doing?

BULL. Excellent. Thank you, sir.

IVAN, BERNIE, TROY *and* BULL *all laugh uproariously.*

JACOB *looks confused.*

TROY. You're a card, Bull. You really are.

BULL. Thank you, sir.

TROY (*to* IVAN). A word.

TROY *exits.*

IVAN, BERNIE and BULL all stop laughing suddenly.

IVAN follows TROY outside.

BERNIE. Mr Bull, perhaps you would be so kind as to start preparing dinner.

BULL. Sir.

BERNIE. An army marches on its stomach, after all.

JACOB. Sir, I just…

IVAN re-enters, ashen-faced.

BERNIE. Well?

A pause. IVAN stares at JACOB.

IVAN. Your orders have been rescinded.

JACOB. I see. And what are my new orders?

Beat.

Sir?

IVAN (*grimly*). You're travelling to the front at first light.

JACOB nods slowly.

JACOB. Thank you, sir.

Blackout.

Scene Four

JACOB *alone, smoking*.

JACOB. The first day's fine. It's all excitement. Everyone wants
to be mates. Friends. You get given all this shiny new gear.
Told it's your sole responsibility to take care of it. That
means cleaning, maintenance, upkeep. Care. Most of us had
never had 'responsibility' before. But then, who does at the
age of fourteen? All we'd known was home. If we were
lucky we'd maybe had a sly drag on a cooch with a couple of
pals or if we were *really* lucky, maybe we'd seen some girl's
sliders up the park. But we were children.

Beat.

And then suddenly, an officer, a man... he's saying that
we're men too. No longer children. We're grown-ups. Time
to face the world. To stand together. And fight. Shoulder to
shoulder. For the good of the Capital State. Help. Assist.

Beat.

Do some good.

A lighting change.

Scene Five

Night.

JACOB *alone*.

IVAN *enters*.

JACOB. He's not as big as I thought he'd be.

IVAN *starts in shock*.

IVAN. Fuck me! You trying to give us an heart attack?!

JACOB *smiles*.

What are you on about now?

JACOB. Troy.

IVAN. What about him?

JACOB. I thought he'd be... you know. *Rotund*.

IVAN. Fat.

JACOB. No, rotund.

IVAN. That means fat.

JACOB. Not necessarily. Rotund can mean something completely different to fat.

IVAN *gets up and goes over to* JACOB.

IVAN. You're saying cos of rumours you may have heard about the son of our leader you expected him to be a fat cunt.

JACOB. No, it's just... everyone said he was... on the rotund side. If there was a spectrum of rotundity, my expectation was that he would be *somewhere* on that spectrum...

IVAN. Fuck me. You don't say things like that. Have you not listened to anything Bernie's said to you?

JACOB. Course. But it's just you and me now.

IVAN *shakes his head, frustrated.*

So. He's lost weight, then. Go on a diet, did he?

IVAN. Oh yeah, he's a regular salad-muncher.

Beat.

He's... been training. This last few years.

JACOB. So he *was* fat before, then?

IVAN. I didn't say that, did I?

JACOB. I just presumed...

IVAN. Yeah? Well, presumption is the mother of all fuck-ups.

JACOB. A-ssumption...

IVAN (*sotto*). SHUTUP!

IVAN *looks upstairs, whispering.*

Look. That one... he's got a *way* about him.

JACOB. A way?

IVAN. Yeah.

JACOB. Right.

IVAN. So…

> IVAN *makes a gesture to suggest the conversation is over and that* JACOB *should be quiet.*

> JACOB *is confused.*

JACOB. When you say 'a way'…?

IVAN. Fuck me.

> *Beat.*

> The way he carries himself… the way he speaks to people. He's… got something behind his eyes. You've met him now. You know what I mean.

> JACOB *nods.*

JACOB. He scares me.

IVAN. I think he scares everyone. Always has. Even when he was…

JACOB. Fat?

IVAN. *Rotund.*

> IVAN *points at* JACOB. *They both smile.*

> Became the thing none of us ever thought he could be. Found his taste for it.

> Like his old man. *Bloodlust.* Some people just have it, don't they.

JACOB. I suppose so.

IVAN. Not that you'd know.

JACOB. Well, I've got my chance to find out now, haven't I?

> *A pause.* IVAN *looks down.*

IVAN. Yeah. Well.

> *Beat.*

You'll be with him and Bernie a few very experienced lads.
It's only a patrol. Routine. The other lot are too far away.

JACOB. Yeah.

IVAN *pats* JACOB *on the shoulder and smiles.*

IVAN. Look, you heard what he said. This could be it. Home,
Jacob! Just… do your duty. Do some good. Help. That's
what we're here for, isn't it?

JACOB. If you say so.

IVAN. Course it is.

JACOB *looks unconvinced.*

What do you think we're doing here?!

JACOB. I'm not sure.

IVAN. Well, I am. We keep the peace. Prevent atrocities. That's
why we're at war.

JACOB. But nobody can remember a time when we weren't at
war. Can you? War has become our status quo.

IVAN. We're soldiers, Jacob. We'd be out of a job if we didn't
have a war to fight, wouldn't we.

JACOB. But why here? Why them?

IVAN. It's just… what needs to be done. We do as we're told.
Obey orders.

JACOB. We're blunt instruments then.

IVAN. No. We're defenders. Defenders of… freedom. Of liberty.

JACOB. Right.

JACOB *looks unsure.*

IVAN *sits him down.*

IVAN. Back when you got your papers… what did it say in big
letters across the top of the first page?

JACOB. Remind me.

IVAN. 'Never shall we succumb to indolence of the heart.'

JACOB. '…indolence of the heart', yeah. I understand.

IVAN. Can we neglect to take care of something that we should? Should we let ourselves succumb to…

JACOB.…acedia.

IVAN. What?

JACOB holds up his book.

IVAN dismisses it with a gesture.

We fight. To protect. That's what I meant, you see… defenders of liberty.

JACOB. Because we can't stand idle when evil deeds are done.

A pause. They stare at one another.

IVAN. Get some sleep.

JACOB nods.

JACOB. Ivan, I know you've gone out of your way to help me and I know that it reflects badly on you if I do anything… irresponsible.

IVAN. Well. You're not going to, are you.

JACOB. No. Course not.

IVAN. Get some rest.

JACOB nods and takes his jacket off.

You'll need it for tomorrow. Tomorrow… well.

JACOB lies down and uses his jacket as a pillow.

Rotund. Ha. Way with words, you've got. A way with bloody words.

IVAN exits back to his room.

Music. A lighting change.

Scene Six

The moon shines through the window.

Footsteps.

HELEN *enters.*

She looks at JACOB.

When JACOB *speaks he does not acknowledge* HELEN.

HELEN. I am nothing, I am just a story told, a tapestry woven,
    a charm uttered, a spell cast.

JACOB. The first day's fine. We stand together. We're shaved
    clean; some of us for the first time. Heads *and* face. Slick
    uniformity. Crisp collars. Starched.

HELEN. You are nothing; you are all fragile, you are all broken,
    all creatures of the earth, all pieces of the same puzzle.

JACOB. The top brass, command, they all tell us we have to do
    our bit. That we're here to help people who are '*oppressed*'.

HELEN. We are nothing; we must be blooded and impure
    before we can return to dust.

JACOB. They talk. We listen. We don't ask questions. We're
    taught how to move, how to stand. How to run, march,
    crouch, crawl, punch, stab, throttle, garotte, kill. We're not
    taught to question. We're taught how to kill.

HELEN. And so kill you must.

   Blackout.

Scene Seven

BULL *sits peeling potatoes.*

IVAN *paces.*

IVAN. They should have been back by now, they definitely should have been back by now. Christ, my nerves. Twenty-odd years in the service. Twenty years and I've never worried like this.

BULL. Have a drink.

IVAN. What?

BULL. Why don't you have a drink?

IVAN. Nah.

BULL. Suit yourself.

A pause.

IVAN *looks at the bottle of Scotch.*

IVAN. I think I'll have a drink.

BULL (*smiling*). Good.

IVAN *pours himself a large drink.*

IVAN. He'll be fine. I know he will. It's experience he so badly needs. Bernie will take care of him.

BULL *nods and smiles.*

It's just… he's not one of them. He's a thinker. He could be useful. In intelligence. But…

BULL. The boy will be fine.

IVAN. Course he will. First day at the front. We've both been through it. Gives you a stoicism. A resolute stoicism. Remember that? Who told you that, eh?

BULL *smiles and points at* IVAN.

IVAN *smiles.*

Yeah. Back then, even you were wet behind the ears. You could barely even tie your laces, could you? Now look at you. Look at the progress you've made.

IVAN *and* BULL *look at one another. Then they look at the potatoes.*

BULL. Well.

They both laugh.

IVAN. Well. Training seems a long time ago now.

BULL. It does.

IVAN. We had some lads, eh? Roddy Cole, John Shollick, remember Bill Brazer?

BULL (*smiling*). Bill Brazer.

IVAN. Whatever happened to old Bill?

BULL. Dead.

IVAN (*nodding*). Mmm. Most of them are, eh? Who else did we have… old Benson, Johnny Bright, Tom Moore, good old Mawsie. Oh… and how could I forget bloody Sixsmith…

BULL *reacts to this name.*

Incompetent bastard. Didn't know his arsehole from his elbow. Had friends in high places, not that it did him much good. Don't matter who your friends are, you still have to go to the front at some point.

Beat.

Bet he was expecting to be an aide to a general or something. Turned out he was the one that needed aid… bloody FIRST AID! Ha!

IVAN *laughs, but* BULL *stops peeling potatoes and pulls a reproachful face.*

IVAN *stops laughing suddenly.*

Sorry. Very bad taste. Shouldn't joke about fallen comrades. It's my nerves. They're making me rather garrulous, you see.

BULL *nods.*

We went over hard, didn't we. 'The first day's fine', as they say. Always is. But then. The chaos. Don't know what we expected. Sixy caught it in the second wave, didn't he. I was forty or fifty metres away from him, but there was no mistaking him. Overweight, bespectacled. Looked more like a priest than a soldier. Still. Least it was quick. And he died a glorious death. For his country.

Beat.

We lost better men than bloody Sixsmith that day. But for some reason, it's him I remember.

BULL *and* IVAN *look at each other.*

The telephone rings making them both jump. BULL *picks it up.*

BULL. Hello?

Beat.

Yes, sir. What's the word?

Beat.

I see.

Beat.

Yes. Yes, he's right here, sir.

BULL *looks to* IVAN *and hands him the phone.*

IVAN. Bernie? Is he alright? The boy?

Beat.

Oh God.

Beat.

Right.

Beat.

And?

Beat.

Really? Excellent.

IVAN*'s relief is palpable.*

Yes. Thanks, Bernie.

IVAN *hands the phone back to* BULL.

BULL. Sir?

Beat.

Yes, sir. Of course, sir.

Beat.

Very good, sir.

Beat.

Indeed I shall, sir.

Laughter can be heard on the other end of the phone.

BULL *hangs up.*

IVAN *takes a deep breath.*

IVAN. There was an ambush. Jacob did very well. A glorious victory for our boys.

This is… a most *satisfactory* outcome, Mr Bull!

Beat.

A celebration!

BULL. Certainly.

IVAN. Some grub, some wine…

BULL. Of course.

IVAN.…nothing too lavish, though. There is a war on, after all.

BULL *nods.*

IVAN *looks pleased with himself and pours another drink.*

Sixsmith. Bloody Sixsmith. Haven't thought about him in a long time.

BULL *finishes peeling a potato. Dries his hands and heads out.*

Strange business, that. Do you remember when we got back…

BULL *stops in the doorway. He does not look at* IVAN.

BULL. Dinner in an hour. Sir.

A pause. BULL *exits.*

IVAN *stares out of the window.*

End of Act One.

ACT TWO

Scene One

BERNIE, JACOB, IVAN *and* BULL *sit around the dining table.*

They are all fairly drunk, except JACOB, *who is sullen and sober.*

JACOB *is bloodied and dirty.*

BULL *and* IVAN *are making a noise to applaud* BERNIE, *who is stood, about to make a toast.*

BERNIE. Today... I have been proved wrong. And I'm not too proud to admit it. Gentlemen, young Jacob here fought with bravery, tenacity and displayed more courage than I have seen in a long time... in a *long* time.

Beat.

So now... we drink to Jacob... patriot, warrior and defender of the Capital State.

ALL. To Jacob!

They all drink except JACOB. *They all applaud.*

IVAN. Excellent!

BERNIE (*to* JACOB). I thought I had the measure of you. Thought I had you good and proper. Never judge a book, eh?

They all laugh except JACOB.

IVAN. It's very good of you to pay such a tribute to the boy.

BERNIE. Not at all.

(*To* JACOB.) It's an honour. And honour is important to us. You see that's why I was being so hard on you yesterday. The honorific system of our military has been in place for many years. The rules of warfare, decorum, respect, a moral code to live by. That's what separates us from them.

JACOB *says nothing*.

An awkward silence.

IVAN. Well. I have to say, Mr Bull: you have excelled yourself.

BULL. Thank you.

BERNIE. Indeed. Bravo.

BULL. Thank you, sir.

> BULL *clears the remaining empty bottles and exits*.

> BERNIE *and* IVAN *stand and stretch their legs*.

BERNIE (*calling after* BULL). More wine! We're celebrating after all, are we not?

> (*To* JACOB.) Come on, lad. Drink up… all this is in your honour.

JACOB. Somehow I don't feel like drinking. Sir.

> BERNIE *and* IVAN *exchange glances*.

IVAN. He's got the Battle Blues, that's all. Don't worry. Everyone gets it the first time.

BERNIE. That's right. Don't feel bad about what you did today. You fought with honour. You did your duty.

> JACOB *says nothing*.

> *A pause*.

> BULL *reappears*.

BULL. I'll have to fetch some from outside, sir. The kitchen is dry.

IVAN (*to* JACOB). Why don't you and Mr Bull go and get some more wine from outside? Just cos you're a war hero, doesn't mean you get to slack off now, does it.

> JACOB *slowly gets up*.

JACOB. Sir.

BERNIE. You bring as much as you can carry, Mr Bull. Which is quite a lot, I imagine?

BULL. Indeed, sir.

    BULL, BERNIE *and* IVAN *laugh a bit too much.*

    JACOB *and* BULL *exit.*

    BERNIE *and* IVAN *stop laughing and stare at one another.*

BERNIE (*quietly*). We're close.

IVAN. We are. We really are.

BERNIE. There's no way we can stay.

IVAN. No. Not after…

BERNIE. No. So we just have to…

    BERNIE *makes a gesture.*

IVAN. Yeah.

    They both smile.

    BERNIE *looks up.*

BERNIE. I always knew she'd be worth it.

IVAN (*uncertain*). She is. Isn't she.

BERNIE. Course she is. The prophecy, eh?

    BERNIE *smiles.*

IVAN. Perhaps.

BERNIE. '*Perhaps?*'

IVAN. It just feels… fragile. The boy. Him. Her. All of it. Feels
    Like we've been… climbing a ladder all these years…

BERNIE. Yeah. And now we're near the top. Aren't we…

IVAN. Yeah. But one wrong move and we're gonna come
    crashing down.

BERNIE. That's why we have to watch our step, don't we. The
    boy especially.

    Beat.

One rung at a time. That's all.

BERNIE *pats* IVAN *on the shoulder.*

They lock eyes.

A pause.

JACOB *and* BULL *re-enter, clutching bottles of wine.*

(*To* JACOB.) Well... how does it feel to have served your first day at the front? To have done your bit, eh?

JACOB. I'm not really sure, sir.

BERNIE. It's tough on you.

JACOB. Sir.

BERNIE. But there's a higher purpose, you see.

TROY *appears at the stairwell, unnoticed.*

He stands, listening silently to their conversation.

JACOB. Is that so, sir.

BERNIE. Of course it is.

JACOB. And just what is that purpose, sir?

IVAN. You fought for the Capital State. For peace... for liberty and freedom.

BERNIE, IVAN *and* BULL *all smile and murmur approvingly.*

JACOB *stares at the table.*

BERNIE. Many a time we've sat at tables like this. We've toasted many victories. We've spilled blood and wine. We've had to lick our wounds and stare at empty places at those tables. Fallen comrades. Friends.

IVAN. Many comrades we've lost over the years. Good men. Valiant men.

IVAN *smiles and turns to* BERNIE.

You know who I was reminded of earlier? Albert Sixsmith.

BERNIE. Albert BLOODY Sixsmith! I've not thought of him in years! Ha! Useless bastard.

IVAN. Weren't he just.

JACOB notices BULL's sullen reaction.

BERNIE. But he served. Brief as his service was, he did his duty and he gave his life so that others may live. Live in peace. And that is our purpose. That's what binds us. The knowledge that we are not men of fortune...

BERNIE checks himself.

...we are not mercenaries. Our purpose is greater. Our purpose... is to bring *peace*.

IVAN nods.

They all look to JACOB for a response, but he remains silent.

IVAN. Mr Bull, a song. Bet you didn't know that Mr Bull is quite the baritone. Oh yes. Fine set of pipes on Mr Bull.

BERNIE. Very fine. Finest in the service.

BULL (*smiling, flattered*). Well.

BERNIE. Go on, Bull. Give us a song. One of the old ones.

BULL and JACOB exchange a look.

BULL hesitates, just for a moment.

BULL nods and begins to sing a sea shanty. It is melancholic, quiet and sentimental.

BULL (*singing*).
    I met a man, down by the sea,
    And of the war he said to me,
    'Come fight for us, come fight my boy.
    Your courage fills my heart with joy.'

BERNIE and IVAN join in, harmonising rather well.

    Met we again, aboard the ship,
    His flask he gave me for a sip.
    He said, 'Be strong, go fight ye well,
    And ye shall have brave tales to tell.'

His face I saw, in fields of blood,
Felled was he, into the mud,
I took his arm and raised him up,
That night shared we, a vict'ry cup.
And as we drank, his eyes grew pale,
He said, 'My boy, you did not fail.
You served your country bold and true.
A hero we have made of you.'

BULL, BERNIE *and* IVAN *all smile at one another and bask in nostalgia for a time.*

JACOB *suddenly stands, scraping his chair across the floor and finally knocking it over with a crash. He laughs viciously as he does so.*

JACOB. That's why we're here then, is it?

Beat.

To be '*heroes*'?

BERNIE. We're here to help. To *assist*.

Beat.

If you'd actually listened to the song, you'd understand that. We help people.

TROY. An interesting theory that, Bernie.

The others all stand to attention suddenly.

BERNIE. Sir, we were… just…

TROY. Yes, I can see that.

Beat.

Go on. What were you saying before?

BERNIE. Just… idle chatter, sir. We were toasting the victory, sir.

TROY. No, no… you were saying 'we help people'.

BERNIE. Well… yes, sir… in a manner of speaking…

TROY. And what manner of speaking is that?

BERNIE. I was just reminding young Jacob of our mission, sir. Ivan and I…

IVAN.…we thought he was… suffering. With a touch of the Battle Blues, sir. And we just wanted to let him know that what he did was… in the name of honour.

TROY. Honour.

BERNIE. Yes.

TROY. I see. And our mission. Remind me what that is again, lads?

IVAN. To fight, sir. To help.

Beat.

To do some…

BERNIE (*proudly*). 'Never shall we succumb to indolence of the heart.'

A pause. JACOB *and* TROY *lock eyes.*

TROY. Mmmmm. Never really understood that, but… sounds nice, don't it, Jacob?

TROY *smiles.*

Basically means… 'we help people'. Right?

JACOB. Do you disagree, sir?

IVAN *and* BERNIE *stare daggers at* JACOB.

TROY. Disagree?

TROY *thinks and edges slowly into the room.*

Well… yes. I suppose I do, Jacob. We've been 'helping' people for thousands of years. Yet we're still at war, aren't we. We still murder each other and ravage each other's women and burn each other alive… sit down, gents, sit down… don't stand there like statues on my account…

The others sit.

…torture each other for information and… blah blah blah blah blah.

Beat.

IT'S EVER SO UNCIVILISED, ISN'T IT?

Beat.

But it just carries on. A cycle is what it is. And what happens in cycles? They go round and round and have no end. People talk about 'stabilisation'… of a truce. But there's no such thing. There are just differing degrees of us all being rather horrible to each other.

TROY *beams and looks at the other men.*

A couple of years back we get called to this building. Horrible. Dirty part of town. Icy rain, pissing in through the smashed windows… and the stink. Disgusting.

Beat.

But there were no bodies anywhere. Or at least, none to be found on initial inspection.

Beat.

We get to this chapel thing. It's dark. Dark as dark can be, but as our eyes adjust, we start to pick out strange shapes with our lanterns, these… faces, rigid in terror and rage. The men. Only the men, mind. About sixteen or seventeen of them… all dead. All against one wall. Chained up. Bodies contorted, limbs broken. But not from torture…

Beat.

And I remember thinking… what horror could make a man break his own bones to be free?

Beat.

But… we turned our lights to the wall opposite and we saw. We saw what that *thing* was. That horror.

TROY *smiles. The others look solemn.*

Their women. Their wives and daughters. Their girls.

Beat.

The men had been made to watch.

Beat.

The women: Stripped. Ravaged. Battered. Torn. Mutilated. Killed.

Beat.

Or at least… that was my assessment of the proceedings.

A pause.

They have no desire to be civilised. They have no desire to reform. They do not. Want. Our help.

A pause.

And we are no different. We're just the same as them.

JACOB. Then why *are* we here, sir?

TROY. To plunder! To exploit those weaker than ourselves and to soak up all we can from them. Deny it as we might; that's why we're here.

TROY *smiles and thinks.*

Couple of years ago, I was in the infirmary with the worst dose of the clap I've ever had…

TROY *feigns embarrassment.*

…I MEAN an innocuous but somewhat concerning virus that was going round…

TROY *winks very obviously at* JACOB.

JACOB *smirks.*

There was this chap who'd had his whole face blown off. Horrible. Looked like a side of ham that had been chewed by a dog. HE WAS IN A RIGHT FUCKING PICKLE, I CAN TELL YOU!

TROY *laughs uproariously.* JACOB *laughs too.*

Right boring bastard. Chat chat chat the whole time, but he only said one thing over and over. Morning and night. Fuck me, I was ready to strangle the cunt by the time I left. But then I got to thinking. And it summed the whole thing up perfectly. That mad chewed-ham-faced bastard, he had us absolutely bang to rights. You know what he said, over and over? 'Pirates. We're pirates.'

Beat.

And he's bang on with that, lads. Skull and crossbones… that's us. You know what pirates are, don't you, Jacob?

JACOB. Yes sir.

TROY. There's just not enough to go around, you see.

JACOB. Enough of what, sir?

TROY. Anything. Enough of anything, Jacob. So we have to take it. All of it.

JACOB. And her too?

A pause.

TROY *looks up.*

TROY. Her? Well. She's everything. She's the moon. Isn't she.

JACOB *and* TROY *lock eyes.*

A pause.

IVAN. Sir, in my opinion…

TROY *silences* IVAN.

TROY. Did I ask you anything, Ivan?

IVAN *looks down.*

A silence.

TROY *laughs.*

Now, that? *That* warranted a slap, Jacob. But I let it slide because I'm feeling somewhat benevolent this evening.

TROY *laughs, yawns and heads to the door.*

Ivan, Bernie. If you'd care to join me, there are preparations to make for the journey ahead. We've had the word and we leave at first light.

The others stay seated.

TROY *looks confused.*

We're going home.

TROY *exits.*

A silence. The others are all stunned.

BERNIE. Home.

IVAN. Home.

IVAN *and* BERNIE *smile and clasp hands.*

Blackout.

Scene Two

JACOB *and* BULL. BULL *is packing and making preparations for the journey.*

JACOB *is sat studying* BULL.

JACOB. Bull, you don't say much.

Beat.

You're a man of few words, are you not.

BULL *smiles.*

I admire that about you. People talk too much.

BULL. Well.

A pause.

JACOB. What happened to him? Sixsmith?

A pause.

BULL (*warning*). It's a long time ago.

JACOB. Please. I'd like to know.

BULL *continues to gather their belongings and pack during the following speech*.

BULL. He died.

BULL *walks away.*

BULL *looks back at* JACOB.

BULL *sighs*.

I remember it quite differently to…

Beat.

It was a very unpleasant death. Very slow. Very painful. Took hours. He was crying out for his mum… crying for anyone. Our orders were to stay put. Eventually… we left him. Didn't have a choice. He was still screaming when…

Beat.

He was… an odd chap. Gentle. Quiet. He always had his head buried in books. Like you. Books about the myths and the prophecies. We all *talked* about them, we all told the stories, but…

Beat.

Well, we thought he really *believed* them. Everyone thought he was cuckoo, until… we got back to base. The day he copped it. And there was his stuff. All boxed up on his bed. His sheets folded like they'd been pressed. Like he knew.

BULL *stands still.*

And above his bunk, he'd written on the wall. Scrawled in red paint.

Beat.

And that was when I realised; he didn't believe a word of it.

BULL *catches himself and gets back to work.*

JACOB. What had he written?

BULL *goes to leave.*

Bull?

BULL *stops in the kitchen doorway.*

A pause.

BULL. *Depravity.* That's all... just... *Depravity.*

A pause.

JACOB (*flat*). That's a great story, Bull, I feel loads better.

BULL. Yeah, well, you asked.

IVAN *comes rushing back in.*

IVAN. Right, executive orders have been given, so let's see them executed.

BULL. Sir.

IVAN. Mr Bull, to the docks, yes?

BULL. Indeed, sir.

BULL *gives* JACOB *a nod.*

JACOB *nods back.*

BULL *leaves.*

IVAN. What the fuck are you playing at?!

JACOB. I'm sorry?

IVAN. Don't play the idiot with me, boy.

JACOB. I'm not the one who got a rather testy rebuke.

IVAN. Well, we can soon address that if you're feeling left out.

JACOB. I killed fifteen people today.

A pause.

IVAN. Well. That's war.

Beat.

I'm sorry.

JACOB. Fifteen different men. Men with families. Children. Dead.

IVAN. Try not to think about it like that.

JACOB. Because they had one colour uniform and I had a different one. That's it.

IVAN. That's not it, though, is it? That's not *it*.

JACOB. Isn't it? What did they do to me? I didn't know those men. We might have been friends. One man I killed, he even looked like me. And you know what I thought, as I killed him?

JACOB *laughs*.

I thought, 'This is weird, must be a bit like how it feels kissing a girl that looks like your sister.'

JACOB *laughs*.

A pause.

IVAN. Look. You're in shock. But you heard him. We're going home. It's over.

JACOB. Over? It isn't over. You think they'll stop? The other lot. After what he's done? This isn't the end, this is just the beginning, isn't it?

IVAN. You shut your fucking mouth. You've been lucky so far, but people don't ask questions like that. Not with him around.

JACOB. Maybe. But in some ways I've got more respect for him than I have for you.

IVAN. What you talking about?

JACOB. They ask us. When we sign up. We all get asked. 'What do you want to do for the Capital State?' And we reply. 'Fight. Help. Assist.'

Beat.

'Do some good.'

JACOB *laughs*.

Do some good. That's so horrific it's funny. (*Mocking, almost singing.*) Indolence of the heart. Responsibility. To stand idly by. To not do what one…

IVAN. Listen to me…

Suddenly there is a huge explosion outside which blows in the window, knocks out the lights and takes them all off of their feet. Gradually the smoke clears and IVAN *manages to get to his feet.*

Jacob?! You okay?!

JACOB (*coughing*). Yeah. I'm fine.

BERNIE staggers in, unhurt but shocked.

BERNIE. Ivan?!

IVAN. Fuck was that?! They can't be that close yet, can they?

BERNIE. Must have been a stray one. Where's Bull?

BULL staggers in, obviously wounded and in quite a large amount of pain.

BULL. Here, sir.

BERNIE. You hurt, Bull?

BULL. Possible fracture of the arm and superficial cuts to the head, sir.

BERNIE. Now's no time for jokes, Bull. We need to get to the docks. Make the arrangements.

BULL. Sir.

BULL goes out.

BERNIE picks up the phone.

BERNIE. It's dead. I'll have to wait till we get down there.

BERNIE heads out.

IVAN (*to* JACOB). Come on.

BERNIE. No. No, the boy stays here.

JACOB *and* BERNIE *lock eyes.*

Best place for him.

IVAN. I think…

BERNIE. That's an order.

IVAN. Sir.

>BERNIE *points at* JACOB, *nods and exits.*

>IVAN *and* JACOB *stare at one another for a time.*

>IVAN *exits.*

>JACOB *looks up.*

>*A lighting change.*

>JACOB *begins to hum the sea shanty.*

Scene Three

The moon is the only light on JACOB.

He continues to hum the song.

One by one, the other men enter and also begin to hum the song.

In an ordered, military fashion, they begin to pack and prepare.

HELEN *speaks the words.*

HELEN.

>I met a man, down by the sea,
>And of the war he said to me,
>'Come fight for us, come fight my boy.
>Your courage fills my heart with joy.'

This packing and preparing begins to alter the stage and it soon becomes the upstairs of the lighthouse.

>Met we again, aboard the ship,
>His flask he gave me for a sip.
>He said, 'Be strong, go fight ye well,
>And ye shall have brave tales to tell.'

*JACOB picks up the knife that BULL was using to peel
potatoes and stares at it for a time.*

His face I saw, in fields of blood,
Felled was he, into the mud,
I took his arm and raised him up,
That night shared we, a vict'ry cup.

All of the men exit but continue to hum the tune.

And as we drank, his eyes grew pale,
He said, 'My boy, you did not fail.
You served your country bold and true.
A hero we have made of you.'

They stop humming.

I am nothing. You are nothing. We are nothing.

Blackout.

Scene Four

A metal bed frame.

HELEN *sits smoking.*

JACOB *enters, very nervously, holding a knife in one hand and
a pomegranate in the other.*

*He stands watching her for a time. He puts the knife in his
pocket.*

JACOB. There was an explosion.

Beat.

I'm here to…

Beat.

They went to find out what's going on.

Beat.

I'm here to keep an eye on you.

HELEN *looks at* JACOB *properly.*

Wait.

Beat.

Why…

Beat.

Yes.

Beat.

Right.

HELEN *turns away from* JACOB.

JACOB *turns to leave but stops.*

You're not… what I expected.

Beat.

Can I get you anything? Some water? Food, maybe?

Beat.

Have you eaten?

Beat.

I could make you something…

A pause. JACOB *looks at* HELEN'*s scars and bruises.*

He's hurt you.

Beat.

We were told…

JACOB *looks away ashamedly.*

You're… HELEN?

Beat.

No, I suppose not.

HELEN (*flat*). Who the fuck are you, then.

JACOB. I'm Jacob.

HELEN. Course you are.

JACOB. There was an operation. To bring you here.

HELEN. Yes, I noticed that.

A pause.

JACOB. I should go. I'm sorry.

HELEN (*quickly*). Want one of my cigarettes?

JACOB. I've got some, thanks.

HELEN. I didn't ask if you had any, I asked if you wanted one of mine.

JACOB. Right. Thanks.

JACOB takes a cigarette.

They both light their cigarettes.

HELEN. They're strong…

JACOB. It's alright. I smoke quite a lot. Apparently it's my 'thing'.

HELEN. Don't say I didn't warn you.

JACOB casually takes a drag and then silently retches.

JACOB (*stifled*). Nice. Smooth.

JACOB coughs hard. They smoke for a time. HELEN studies JACOB for a time.

HELEN. How old are you?

JACOB. Twenty.

HELEN. Twenty. You're nearly the same age as him. Yet you seem so much younger.

Beat.

Seventeen.

JACOB. I'm sorry?

HELEN. I'm seventeen. You were about to ask me how old I am. I'm seventeen.

JACOB *looks confused*.

What.

JACOB. No, nothing. Seventeen. That's a good age to be.

HELEN. Why is seventeen a good age to be.

JACOB. Age of maturity. For men. At least, it is where I come from.

Beat.

There's a big ceremony, usually. To celebrate.

HELEN. Maturity.

JACOB. Yes.

HELEN. Men never really reach maturity, do they. They just look older and learn bigger words.

JACOB. Right. Are you hungry?

HELEN. I told you, I'm fine.

HELEN *just looks at him*.

The sound of a far-away battle can be heard.

HELEN *studies the cigarette in her hand*.

Have you ever looked close up at one of these? It looks like the earth burning... like a tiny version of our world cracking and sizzling in the flames.

(*Deliberately sinister*.) Like the end has come...

HELEN *laughs at herself*.

JACOB (*confused*). Yeah... yeah, I should quit.

HELEN. Why?

JACOB. It's pretty bad for you.

HELEN. Why do it then.

JACOB. Passes the time, I suppose. Just like anything else. We need something to occupy us, don't we?

HELEN. Men do, it would seem.

JACOB. We all have our vices.

Beat.

My friend says… we all have to cope somehow.

HELEN. Your friend is right.

Beat.

Why did you come up here?

JACOB. Just… to make sure you're alright. The explosion…

HELEN. No, you're here to do something, aren't you.

JACOB. Am I?

HELEN. I'm not sure what… not yet. I don't know what sort you are.

JACOB. What sort? I'm just keeping an eye on you. As I said.

HELEN. No. You're here to do something. Something '*important*'.

JACOB. What?

HELEN. There are men who want to do the worst, the unspeakable. There are men who do the same thing, but apologise for it and want your forgiveness. There are men who stand in the corner and say nothing; but they also DO nothing. Then there are men who think they 'understand'… but want a medal for NOT being a fucking psychopath. If I had to guess, I'd say you're the latter.

JACOB *stares at her.*

JACOB. You don't know anything about me.

HELEN. Maybe I do. Maybe I don't.

HELEN *turns away from him.*

A pause.

JACOB. And you? Why are you here?

HELEN. Don't you know?

JACOB. I know what I've heard.

HELEN *smiles*.

HELEN. Oh yeah. The 'prophecy'. Bet you're a bit disappointed, eh?

JACOB *doesn't know what to say.*

JACOB. I shouldn't be here.

JACOB *goes to leave.*

HELEN. What's your story?

JACOB. What? What story?

HELEN. All the men I've met have stories. That's where the myths come from. It doesn't matter how heroic or how barbaric, whether they're real or made up, they're all just branches of the same enormous tree, creaking under the weight of this epic, fantastical *myth*.

JACOB *nods*.

JACOB. They all talk about the myths. About their lives and their experiences.

HELEN. Why are men are so infatuated with their *experiences*? What they've seen. What they've done. The most interesting thing about a man is something that he's *never* done.

JACOB. Are you sure you're not hungry? I brought... whatever this is. Some sort of... fruit, I suppose?

JACOB *holds up the pomegranate.*

HELEN. It's a pomegranate. Have you never had a pomegranate before?

JACOB. No. Can't say I have.

HELEN. They're good. Cut it open.

JACOB *takes out his knife and halves the pomegranate.*

JACOB. Fancy that. Little red berries on the inside.

HELEN. My people say that a pomegranate is good luck. It's a sign of fertility. They give them to women at weddings, as a blessing for a large and healthy family.

JACOB sniffs the fruit.

JACOB. Smells good. What bits of it do you eat?

HELEN. Just the berries. The flesh gets discarded.

HELEN tosses her hair dramatically.

Like so much of life.

HELEN laughs.

JACOB. Right.

JACOB attempts to cut all of the berries into a bowl but the ensuing mess leaves him with bright-red pomegranate juice all over his hands.

Messy, isn't it?

HELEN takes the other half of the pomegranate and the knife.

JACOB is alarmed by the situation.

HELEN scrunches the pomegranate and then continuously bangs it hard with the knife handle until all of the seeds come out.

HELEN. Still messy. Just faster.

She hands the knife and the pomegranate back to JACOB.

JACOB offers the berries to HELEN who shakes her head. He eats some of the berries.

JACOB. Nice. They're sweet. Well, that's something new. I've eaten a pomegranate.

JACOB smiles at HELEN. She does not smile back.

HELEN sits, facing away from JACOB.

JACOB stands behind HELEN, staring at the red liquid on his hands. He holds the knife.

HELEN. Apparently when I was little, I used to have bright-red cheeks. So my mother used to call me her 'Little Pomegranate'.

JACOB. She sounds nice. Your mother.

HELEN. She was.

Beat.

I'm not going to tell you about her so don't ask.

An explosion, closer than before. JACOB *goes to the window.*

He cleans his hands.

JACOB. They're getting closer.

HELEN. Really.

JACOB *thinks.*

JACOB. I was at the front today, I did… things. I killed people.

HELEN *(shrugs).* Just another experience. Same as the others.

JACOB. Well, you said it yourself earlier: men need something to occupy them. It would seem that war is our occupation.

HELEN. Quite an occupation.

JACOB. Indeed it is.

HELEN. And what part do you play in all this?

JACOB. I'm in military intelligence.

HELEN *looks* JACOB *up and down.*

HELEN. Things are worse than I thought.

They both smile.

JACOB. I studied for a long time to get in. Worked hard. Thought I could make a difference.

Beat.

I read a lot of books, to try and… get some perspective. But the more you read, the more you see…

HELEN….the irony of the phrase 'military intelligence'?

JACOB. I suppose so.

HELEN. My people have it too. It's like the blind leading the blind. I'd laugh if it wasn't…

JACOB. Yeah.

HELEN. Greed and arrogance, that's all it is. Possession.

JACOB. I'm sure it doesn't start that way.

HELEN. Maybe not. But in the end it's all about possession. Even me. I'm just another trophy for them to fight over. I'm no different.

JACOB. You are. You're everything.

HELEN. I hate to be the bearer of bad news. I'm just like you. Or him. Or anyone. I'm nobody. I'm nothing. Same as you. We… are *nothing*.

JACOB. You still matter.

HELEN turns to JACOB suddenly, desperately.

HELEN. Well, if that's true then you have a choice to make, don't you.

JACOB turns away.

JACOB. You know what the old saying is? Where I come from? 'We help. We assist. We do some good.' And we *really* believe it. We believe we're helping.

HELEN (*pleading*). Belief is not the same as truth, though, is it. We can believe anything we like as long as we don't stop to question it.

Beat.

But a belief unquestioned is a story half-written.

JACOB. And how does this story end?

HELEN. The same as all the others, I'm afraid.

JACOB. Where I come from, stories usually have happy endings.

HELEN. It depends upon your perspective, no? Truth isn't important in a story, is it... truth can very easily become like a guest who has outstayed their welcome. What matters is that you are happy with what *you believe* to be true. That's how people live like this.

Beat.

'We all have to cope, somehow.' Your friend said that. It's the saddest thing. The saddest thing.

A pause.

An explosion, closer than before.

There isn't much time.

JACOB. I know.

HELEN *looks scared, desperate.*

HELEN. What have they told you about me?

JACOB. It sounds childish.

HELEN *stares at him.*

They call you the moon. I don't understand why. They say that you are...

HELEN *nods.*

HELEN. It's just another story.

HELEN *satirises her story as she tells it.*

He came to pay tribute. He came with gifts and servants and weapons and smiles. I was no more than a child, but I could feel his eyes on me, even then. They bored into me. My father; he knew. No one knows an evil man's mind better than another evil man. He poisoned everyone with his words.

HELEN *laughs despondently and stops the satire.*

She looks down sadly.

The stories, they seem harmless. You all stare out to sea and wonder who am, what I am. I've become an obsession. For men. But I'm just a distraction.

Beat.

The hearts of men are weak, after all. They don't stop to listen
or ask why, they prevail in the pursuit of heroism, of triumphs
and victories. Do you ever question the cost, the worth?

Beat.

This. This is the cost. Me and millions like me. The beaten
and the broken. The lost.

Beat.

I still hear your songs in my dreams; songs of camaraderie
and 'courage'. I hear you all bask in the warm glow of your
exploits. The battle won with daring and valour, your
dignified enemies conquered.

HELEN *stares at* JACOB.

There is nothing… NOTHING that the furies of this world;
whatever gods there are, whatever spirits above or below
us… there is no grief that could be greater than that which
you men have created for yourselves. You men in your…

HELEN *searches for the word.*

JACOB. Depravity.

HELEN *and* JACOB *lock eyes.*

HELEN. How's that for a fucking story?

JACOB (*under his breath*). A belief unquestioned is a story
half-written.

HELEN *takes* JACOB*'s face in her hands.*

HELEN. The war that will be fought for me will be just another
terrible war; fought for pride, greed and vengeance. The
same as all the others.

JACOB *steps away from* HELEN, *utterly torn.*

He stands clutching the knife tightly.

There's nothing else to say. I've told you my story.

A pause. JACOB *is conflicted but then nods.*

JACOB. Yes.

JACOB *turns to leave.*

HELEN. So tell me yours.

JACOB *stops.*

JACOB *turns back.*

JACOB. The first day's fine.

Blackout.

Scene Five

The downstairs of the lighthouse.

Wind and rain lash at the windows.

The battle can be heard in the distance.

JACOB *sits smoking and staring at the cover of his book. He seems detached and distant.*

IVAN *enters, soaked through.*

JACOB *and* IVAN *look at each other for a time.*

IVAN. Not got the fire on?

JACOB *and* IVAN *both look at the fire and then each other.*

JACOB. To state the obvious, Ivan, no. I haven't.

IVAN. No need to be a cunt about it.

Beat.

And don't forget who your senior officer is, here.

JACOB *nods and smiles.*

JACOB (*genuinely*). I'm sorry, sir. You're absolutely right.

IVAN *looks pleased.*

IVAN. Good. Well. Anyway, the news is that the other lot are closer than we thought. Probably not close enough, but still. There's been some fighting. And there'll be more.

IVAN *smiles*.

But we'll be gone. Home.

IVAN *starts to get excited, giddy like a child*.

You packed? Ready?

IVAN *seems disappointed by* JACOB*'s lack of enthusiasm*.

JACOB *says nothing, but simply stares at the cover of his book*.

Are you hearing a bloody word I'm saying? We are LEAVING. I swear…

JACOB. I finished my book.

IVAN (*confused*). Right. I see. Any good?

JACOB. Yes it was. Listen to this.

(*Reading*.) 'Those who have sinned by acedia find their everlasting home in the fifth circle of the Inferno. They are plunged in the same black bog with the Wrathful, and their sobs and words come bubbling up to the surface.'

JACOB *smiles*.

IVAN. Very nice. What's that mean then?

JACOB. I'm not really sure. Sounds quite apt though, doesn't it?

IVAN *eyeballs* JACOB *for a time, then decidedly changes the subject*.

IVAN. See, I'm right about that sitting-down thing, aren't I? Eh?

JACOB. Yes. I think I shall definitely do more of it.

IVAN. Oh will you indeed?

JACOB. I think so, yes.

IVAN. Right. Well, just remember, only an appropriate amount is good for a young man.

JACOB. What's an appropriate amount?

IVAN. Well, it depends on your age.

JACOB. Really?

IVAN. As you get older, the appropriate ratio of sitting-to-standing starts to sway in favour of sitting. When you get to my age, you can sit whenever you bloody well like. Speaking of which...

IVAN gestures. JACOB gets up and lets IVAN sit.

JACOB and IVAN laugh. They're excitable with nervous energy.

Ah! There we go.

JACOB. So when does this shift happen?

Beat.

How am I supposed to know when I'm allowed to sit and when I'm supposed to stand? I'm not entirely clear of the rules.

IVAN. You just know. Trust your instincts.

JACOB. My instincts?!

They laugh.

IVAN. Yeah!

JACOB. Right.

More laughter.

You ever eaten a pomegranate, Ivan?

IVAN. Eh? You what?

They laugh at the absurdity of the question.

JACOB. A pomegranate. Ever eaten one?

IVAN. Can't say I have, Jacob, no!

JACOB. Oh!

IVAN looks confused, but they both laugh, becoming more hysterical as the conversation goes on.

IVAN. Sorry, did I miss something?!

JACOB. No! Haha!

IVAN. Right! Well, why not ask me some more obscure and irrelevant questions?

They laugh throughout.

Care to know if I've ever played hopscotch? Interested in my
thoughts on underwater plant life? He's gone BARMY!!
Haha!

JACOB. A pomegranate's quite a thing, Ivan.

IVAN. You been at my whisky?

More laughter.

JACOB. It's not just the eating of it, mind. It's the seeding of it.
Extracting the seeds. You split it down the middle with a big
sharp knife.

IVAN (*to himself*). He's lost it. He's lost the bloody plot.

Beat.

Are you actually listening to yourself?

More laughter.

JACOB. The juice starts to flow when you scrunch that halved
fruit in your fist and hit it…

IVAN. That's it. I'm having him committed! He's a certified
bloody loony!! Haha!

JACOB. The fruit bleeds, the arils, that's what they call the
seeds, they pop out like little rubies and the white pulp splits
like… like an earthquake. It's quite a beautiful thing, Ivan…

IVAN *still laughs but starts to become more and more
confused.*

IVAN. STOP!

JACOB.…to take those pomegranates and bleed them and rip
them to pieces and take those beautiful, juicy jewels and do
with them what we will, leaving leftovers of nothing more
than broken skin and carved innards and a trail of bright-red
liquid dripping from your hands…

IVAN. Pomegranates. Right, okay.

I see…

IVAN *looks uneasy and keeps looking to the door.*

JACOB. They're important over here. They have… cultural
significance. They're a symbol of fertility. And of goodness.
Some people think that they can make you invincible. Some
people call them 'the fruit of life'… because they think there
are three hundred and sixty-five seeds in each one. SO many
myths about one fruit, I couldn't believe it.

(*Suddenly vicious.*) QUITE A FUCKING METAPHOR,
THAT, ISN'T IT, IVAN!

They stop laughing.

They stare at each other.

I ate one today. My first ever pomegranate. She didn't want
any, but I enjoyed it.

IVAN. What? *She?* What are you talking about?

A pause.

JACOB. I didn't understand. I didn't understand what she was.
The stories, the prophecies, the myths… they're just…

IVAN *gets up and starts rushing around, apoplectic, but
unsure what to do.*

IVAN. What the fuck have you… what have you done…

IVAN *goes to the stairs and looks up, terrified.*

IVAN *looks back at* JACOB, *before suddenly forcing himself
to rush up the stairs.*

JACOB. It's for the best. You have to understand.

Music; it is epic but sad and reflective.

HELEN *appears. She and* JACOB *look at one another.*
IVAN *does not acknowledge her presence.*

HELEN. A little girl sits and plays and tangles her hair in
wreaths of ringlets and dreams of having angel wings. She
isn't anyone. She is nothing. We are all nothing.

Beat.

But we are free.

JACOB *and* HELEN *smile.*

HELEN *is gone.*

The music continues to underscore.

JACOB *walks to the window and stares out. He lights a cigarette and listens to the battle for a time.*

IVAN *comes back down.*

IVAN *stares at* JACOB, *takes out a knife and points it at him.*

IVAN. I'll kill you dead where you fucking stand.

JACOB. In time you'll understand.

IVAN *looks devastated.*

IVAN. You don't realise what you've done.

IVAN *tries to comprehend the gravity of the situation.*

We were going HOME, Jacob! HOME!

JACOB (*gestures out of the window*). You hear that? That's all because of her. It's all for one person. For nothing.

IVAN. You think you fucking understand everything because you've read books about war and politics and history and the like, but you don't understand *people*. You don't understand it here. What it means to be here, to serve. To commit to the cause. To really fucking believe…

JACOB. *Believe?* Believe in what?

IVAN. In the cause. In our cause.

JACOB. But have you ever really thought about it? Belief. What is that. 'A belief unquestioned is a story half-written.' She told me that. Good, isn't it?

IVAN. *Good…* is what we're here to do. To help.

Beat.

Why? Why…

JACOB. Raptus? Depravity? Acedia?

IVAN. They're just words. They don't mean anything.

JACOB. And neither does she. She's nothing. We are *nothing*.

IVAN. That's it? You're mad. Fucking mad.

JACOB. Mad? Mad is committing your life to destruction because you're told to. Mad is doing everything someone else wants you to do without ever stopping and asking yourself whether you should or not. That's mad.

IVAN. You know nothing about it.

JACOB. Tell me that I'm wrong. That you genuinely believe us to be doing *good*.

IVAN. What choice do we have? How long does something have to go on before we help? What's the body count? You'd let a man beat another man in front of you, would you? And then watch as another man joins in and they beat him together? And then a third and fourth and more and more? Until they're beating more people. Where do you draw the line and say 'no more'? I don't fucking know.

JACOB. I don't know either. All I know is this: there must be another way.

IVAN. Another way? Like what?! We see people in trouble and we come to their aid. Yes, people get hurt along the way. There are mistakes; civilians feel the burden of occupation. Many great men are lost...

JACOB. WOMEN.

IVAN. Of course *women*. It's collateral damage!

The phrase hangs in the air. They eyeball one another.

A pause.

JACOB. I don't accept that.

IVAN. Well, acceptance is part of what we do.

JACOB. Do you not see how absurd that is? We don't question anything, we just accept what we're told. We're the intelligence division, but nobody here fucking KNOWS anything!

Beat.

It's wrong. That's what I believe to be true now, Ivan. That is what I BELIEVE. And a belief unquestioned is a story half-written, you can't argue with that.

IVAN *paces, trying to process it all.*

It was the only way, Ivan. To break the status quo. To break *our* status quo.

IVAN. Well done. Jacob the fucking hero.

JACOB. You still don't see. She saved us. All of us.

BERNIE *and* BULL *come barrelling through the door, both out of breath.*

BERNIE. Well, come on, why are you…

IVAN *and* BERNIE *exchange a look.*

BERNIE *looks at the door to upstairs and back at* IVAN.

IVAN *shakes his head.*

BERNIE *goes upstairs quickly.*

IVAN (*to himself*). One rung at a time. One rung at a time.

BERNIE *comes back ashen-faced.*

BERNIE *and* IVAN *look at one another.*

BERNIE *and* BULL *look at one other.*

BULL *looks distraught.*

BERNIE. Well.

IVAN. I think we should…

BERNIE. Quiet.

Beat.

Jacob.

JACOB. Sir.

BERNIE. You have made yourself a traitor.

JACOB. It would seem so, sir.

BERNIE. I admire your honesty.

JACOB. It doesn't matter to me any more, sir.

BERNIE. That is a shame. It really is.

Beat.

You know what the punishment for treason is, don't you?

JACOB. I do.

BERNIE. Very well.

BERNIE *gestures to the door.*

Mr Bull? If you would be so kind.

BULL *stands still.*

BULL. Depravity. Nothing but depravity.

BERNIE. MR BULL!

BULL *takes his knife out and walks towards* JACOB.

In an instant, IVAN *points his knife at* BULL *and* BERNIE *responds by pointing his knife at* IVAN.

IVAN. Don't you fucking…!!!   BERNIE. Ivan!!!

A tense stand-off ensues.

Explosions very nearby.

TROY *enters and stands amongst them.*

A pause.

More explosions, even closer.

TROY *eyeballs* JACOB. JACOB *is defiant.*

TROY. Jacob. What have you done.

JACOB (*relishing every word*). Now… now we are sullen in the black mire.

JACOB *smiles.*

TROY *looks at* IVAN, *then* BERNIE, *then* BULL. *Huge explosions very nearby.*

The music swells.

TROY. Shall we, boys?

Nobody moves.

Blackout.

The End.

A Nick Hern Book

The Acedian Pirates first published in Great Britain in 2016 as a paperback original by Nick Hern Books Limited, The Glasshouse, 49a Goldhawk Road, London W12 8QP, in association with Tara Finney Productions and Theatre503, London

Cover design by Adam Loxley

Designed and typeset by Nick Hern Books, London
Printed in Great Britain by Mimeo Ltd, Huntingdon, Cambridgeshire PE29 6XX

A CIP catalogue record for this book is available from the British Library

ISBN   978 1 84842 614 6